Kindled in the Flame
The Apocalyptic Scene in
D.H. Lawrence

Studies in Modern Literature, No. 21

A. Walton Litz, General Series Editor

Professor of English
Princeton University

Keith Cushman

Consulting Editor for Titles on D.H. Lawrence
Professor of English
University of North Carolina at Greensboro

Other Titles in This Series

Kindled in the Flame
The Apocalyptic Scene in D.H. Lawrence

by
Sarah Urang

UMI RESEARCH PRESS
Ann Arbor, Michigan

Copyright © 1983
Sarah Urang
All rights reserved

Produced and distributed by
UMI Research Press
an imprint of
University Microfilms International
Ann Arbor, Michigan 48106

Library of Congress Cataloging in Publication Data

Urang, Sarah.
Kindled in the flame.

(Studies in modern literature ; no. 21)
Revision of thesis—Columbia University, 1980.
Bibliography: p.
Includes index.
1. Lawrence, D. H. (David Herbert), 1885–1930—
Religion and ethics. 2. Bible in literature. 3. Apocalyptic
literature—History and criticism. I. Title. II. Series.
PR6023.A93Z938 1983   823'.912   83-1380
ISBN 0-8357-1436-5

For Gunnar

Contents

Acknowledgments

There are several people to whom I particularly offer my thanks for help with this book in its original form as a dissertation: to Professor George Stade, of Columbia University, for valuable criticism and advice on the manuscript at various stages of its writing; to Professor Daniel Dodson, also of Columbia University, for reading and commenting on the manuscript at a later stage; also to my parents John and Olwen Horton, for their continuing support and interest.

My greatest debt is to my husband, Gunnar Urang. Had it not been for his unfailingly generous encouragement, this project would have foundered long ago. Unstinting of his time and attention, he initiated and shared in countless discussions on Lawrence, and read and criticized my argument throughout the various stages of its development.

But there is a flame or a Life Everlasting wreathing through the cosmos for ever and giving us our renewal, once we can get in touch with it.

It is when men lose their contact with the eternal life-flame, and become merely personal, things in themselves, instead of things kindled in the flame, that the fight between man and woman begins....

And then there is nothing for men to do but to turn back to life itself.... How to be renewed, reborn, revivified? That is the question men must ask themselves, and women too.

—"The Real Thing"

1

Introduction: Lawrence's Rhetoric of Vision

> I was brought up on the Bible, and seem to have it in my bones. From early childhood I have been familiar with Apocalyptic language and Apocalyptic images: not because I spent my time reading Revelation, but because I was sent to Sunday School and to Chapel, to Band of Hope and to Christian Endeavour, and was always having the Bible read at me or to me.[1]

Lawrence wrote these words in 1929, in an introduction to Frederick Carter's "The Dragon of the Apocalypse," a manuscript which had excited him very much.[2] Carter's interpretation of the book of Revelation was unorthodox: he saw the narrative as a disguised star-myth, an astrological scheme which described the interpenetration of man and the natural world. Carter puts it thus, in the later version of his argument, *The Dragon of Revelation:*

> Man—little man—is the Microcosm in whom exists the potential, the very form and pattern of the great world. The great world—the universe—is the Macrocosm, the vast and Heavenly Man—the Adam Kadmon of Jewish mysticism. So it comes that man may seek and find within himself the very realm of heaven and find it there only.[3]

The argument of *Dragon of Revelation* is cloudy; Lawrence acknowledges, in his discussion of the manuscript of the earlier work "The Dragon of the Alchemists," that much of it is confused and not very interesting. Nor does Lawrence subscribe to Carter's thesis that the book of Revelation is a star myth. But this does not matter to him. What he does find in Carter's interpretation is a freeing of the biblical symbols and events; the imagination is released to contemplate them afresh. Lawrence writes of this effect:

> A real release of the imagination renews our strength and our vitality, makes us feel stronger and happier. Scholastic works don't release the imagination: at the best, they satisfy the intellect, and leave the body an unleavened lump. But when I get the release into the zodiacal cosmos my very feet feel lighter and stronger, my very knees are glad.

What the Apocalypse means matters less. "All one cares about is the lead, the lead that the symbolic figures give us, and their dramatic movement: the lead, and where it will lead us to."[4]

Yet Lawrence has his own version of the "meaning" of Revelation, one which he sets forth in the earlier introduction to Carter's book, an introduction that proved to be too long and was published posthumously as a separate essay, *Apocalypse*. Lawrence argues in *Apocalypse* that the Christian book of Revelation is a later, corrupted version of an original account of the initiation ritual surrounding the worship of an Eastern Mediterranean mystery goddess, such as Cybele or Artemis. The later, moral disposition of the work is a reprehensible overlay with which Lawrence has no patience.

> The weak and pseudo-humble are going to wipe all worldly power, glory, and riches off the face of the earth, and then they, the truly weak, are going to reign. It will be a millennium of pseudo-humble saints, and gruesome to contemplate.[5]

Nevertheless, as Lawrence said in his shorter introduction, the work still lives in the power of ancient symbol and in the drama which provides a model of psychic processes that lie still within us.

From so longstanding a familiarity with the book of Revelation, one would expect Lawrence's work to reflect the matter and imagery of Apocalypse. Many critics have mentioned the Bible as a source of Lawrence's diction and metaphor, but few have developed a study of the consequences of Lawrence's profound acquaintance with the idea of Apocalypse, as it might manifest itself in the structure and imagery of his own narrative. Exceptions include Frank Kermode, whose book *D.H. Lawrence* and essay "Lawrence and the Apocalyptic Types"[6] explore apocalyptic as a major expression of Lawrence's creative imagination, and L.D. Clark, whose essay "The Apocalypse of Lorenzo"[7] provides an excellent introductory overview of Lawrence's apocalyptic thought, centering on the two periods of Lawrence's life when such concerns came most urgently to the fore in him—that is, during the First World War and from 1923 to 1929, when he had read Carter's "Dragon of the Apocalypse" and was pondering his own introduction to Carter's work. William Barr, in an unpublished dissertation, also attempts to review the development of Lawrence's use of the book of Revelation, seeing apocalypse as a "central metaphor" for the writer as well as a vehicle for expressing an attitude towards "dominant tendencies in contemporary civilization."[8]

Others have examined the history of Lawrence's ideas regarding social change, the relationship of the self to society, and the Utopian dream. These writers incorporate in their work aspects of Lawrence's apocalyptic thinking. Two particularly thorough and penetrating analyses of Lawrence's thought are Eugene Goodheart's *The Utopian Vision of D.H. Lawrence* and Baruch Hochman's *Another Ego*, which builds on and finely develops Goodheart's study.[9]

My intention is to follow out a rather different line. Since Lawrence is a writer who, by his own avowal, found the fluid and the changing, rather than the fixed or static, close to his own creative mode, I should like to concentrate on what Lawrence's knowledge of the Apocalypse does to the articulation of his plots, the changing imagery of his fiction, the texture of the novel: that which might be considered the *mythos* of his narrative. I shall try to see how apocalyptic concerns are expressed characteristically within certain of the major novels, and what differences or developments might take place from novel to novel in the use of apocalyptic material. Since I attempt to look at the apocalyptic moment within the running stream of the narrative, I center on analysis of specific scenes within the novels, remembering that "all things flow and change, and even change is not absolute. The whole is a strange assembly of apparently incongruous parts, slipping past one another."[10] I use Lawrence himself as his most interesting critic, drawing on his discursive writings as illuminative of the novels.

Although of much less value than soundings in the specific narratives themselves, some general characteristics can be seen in Lawrence's use of the apocalyptic, and certain developments can be outlined. In *The Rainbow,* where this pattern first becomes significant, apocalyptic encounter occurs primarily between individuals. Lawrence's characters typically find themselves in an emotional confrontation from which they emerge with a sense, not only of greater understanding of their connection with each other, but of that understanding being so sure and so vivid that it seems as if the former self had been destroyed in a kind of psychic conflagration. The event is characterized by its suddenness, its completeness, and by an apparent dissolution of the processes of gradual understanding with which we are familiar. The apocalyptic encounter between individuals is amplified in *Women in Love* by Lawrence's persuasion, fostered through the early part of World War I, that his novel takes place in a fictive time analogous to that period described in the Bible as the Last Days. The apocalyptic Day of the Lord is imminent; it is imperative that individuals decide for righteousness, or they will find destruction. The characters in the novel are caught up in a desperate interrogation of their being: every action depends upon a radical moral—or, more accurately, an ontological—choice. The various scenes, therefore, offer themselves as presenting an immanent Last Judgment, and the everyday actions of the characters seem to have eschatological importance. Choices which in *The Rainbow* were more narrowly personal broaden their implications so that they now incorporate and will decide the destiny of the culture.

In the middle novels—*Aaron's Rod, The Plumed Serpent,* and *Kangaroo*—Lawrence considers the cultural situation more directly, exploring in *Kangaroo,* and especially in *The Plumed Serpent,* the possibility of apocalyptic regeneration through religious/political revolution.[11] In the major fiction after this period—*The Man Who Died* and *Lady Chatterley's Lover*—Lawrence finds a chastened understanding of renewal. He returns to the meeting of individuals, though his regard is now suffused with the sadness of disappointed hope in any rapid cultural renewal. His hope—and it does remain as an article of faith held to with a fragile tenacity—is in the power of individual change as germinal of social reconstruction: what might be called the visionary's holographic sense of reality.

This dialectical movement between inner and outer concern is not unlike the drama of apocalyptic renovation documented by M.H. Abrams in *Natural Supernaturalism*. For Wordsworth, Blake, and Shelley, apocalypse was to take place within the world of society; they acclaimed the American and French revolutions as presaging the imminent liberation of oppressed man. However, a gradual disillusionment with the effects of social revolution brought about in those poets a turning inward in order to seek renewal within the mind itself, through a transformed perception which would create the world anew in primordial grace.[12]

The tradition on which Lawrence and other modern apocalyptists draw is one originally not focused directly on psychological states or processes, but detailing divine intervention in the human society and the natural world. The book of Revelation, written late in the first century A.D., stands within an already long history of Jewish apocalypse. During the Babylonian captivity, in the sixth century B.C., the people of Israel, lamenting that their God was far off and deaf to their cries for deliverance, heard their prophets declaiming judgment, declaring that the people's slavery was God's retribution for sinfulness. But at the same time another order of prophecy spoke of a divine plan in which present captivity was merely the intended suffering of a people who would eventually witness the downfall of their enemies. God would at last overthrow the oppressors and return his people to the land of Israel. There is obscure mention of the end of the world and dramatizations of universal cataclysm. In Ezekiel mysterious creatures from folklore—four-faced cherubim, strange wheels, precious stones—accompany prophecies of destruction and of return to the homeland. "I will even gather you from the people and assemble you out the countries where ye have been scattered and I will give you the land of Israel" (Ezekiel 11:17).

In the Book of Daniel a vision of apocalypse purports to have been written during the Babylonian captivity, but in fact probably derives from a much later date, around the second century B.C., during the Maccabean revolt. By this time apocalyptic literature had accumulated a formidable array of imagery: beasts, such as the eagle, the lion, the leopard, and the bear; a complicated numerology; and—just as in the book of Revelation—the appearance of the Ancient of Days.

The writer of the New Testament book of Revelation, a Christian prophet named John—a native of Ephesus—created his vision of destruction and renovation during the reign of the emperor Domitian, from the island of Patmos where, it is likely, he had been exiled for refusing to worship the emperor. His letter, addressed to the seven young churches of Asia Minor, envisions with lurid satisfaction the imminent downfall of the Roman Empire and a world remade for the redeemed, free from possibility of oppression and slavery, perfect for ever. [13]

The vision is caught up with the historical moment, in that it is designed to give courage to the beleaguered Christian communities of Asia Minor. But at the same time, in the fantastic and complicated imagery with which the writer characterizes God's overthrow of his enemies, the letter more generally postulates a divine power able magically to destroy a hopelessly corrupt world. By incomprehensible agency God can renovate a society which has gone wrong far beyond the power of human restoration. Apocalypse gives comfort to a people who can see no way out; at a stroke God will destroy all enemies and return the world to the oppressed.

Although the literal apocalyptic hope is confined now to minor sects, it has flourished in the past as a more pervasive belief, specifically at times of great suffering for those who consider themselves of the elect and therefore feel this hardship as especially unmerited. Such was the case among the Israelites in captivity and the Christians under Domitian. Norman Cohn, in *The Pursuit of the Millennium,* vividly documents the successive waves of millennarian movements that swept Northern Europe between the end of the eleventh and the first half of the sixteenth centuries. He points out that chiliasm flourished during periods when the poor saw their deprivation as the denial of a prosperity rightfully theirs; typically such movements arose at times, and in areas, of what today we might call "rising expectations."[14]

The apocalyptist, then, evisions a cataclysmic destruction of the present corrupt world and its replacement by a new order formed in the image of fulfilled desire. Such is the image of comfort, protection, and peace described in the book of Revelation, especially in chapters 21 and 22. The apocalyptic vision therefore arises from a sensibility shaped by two convictions: one, that deep-rooted corruption is endemic in the world, and the second, that joy is possible and the rightful state for man. L.D. Clark puts it thus: "The underlying reason for the apocalyptist's desire for the destruction of his surroundings is that these surroundings stifle his deep yearnings for a glorious life."[15] Indeed, according to biblical history, apocalypse can only be understood through the image of paradise. The renovated world is Eden restored, and paradise itself can only be known through its loss. Not until angels with flaming swords bar access to Eden does Eden come into being.

And so Lawrence's work takes on an apocalyptic dimension when his vision of paradise has to make sense of an equally vivid apprehension of the fallen world of loss and degradation. What, then, is the image of paradise in a writer who so distrusted the static, the eternally perfected? "If you're a novelist," Lawrence answers, "you know that paradise is in the palm of your hand, and on the end of your nose, because both are alive; and alive, and man alive."[16]

Even in his earliest writing Lawrence shows a special awareness that "all things that live are amazing" and that in this is our first satisfaction; and he reveals an unusual capacity for transmitting the extraordinary sense of life that he finds in the transaction of day to day events. *Sons and Lovers*, for instance, owes its density of substance to this power; and such concentration, which is essentially a meditative activity, results in the intense realization of some of the poems of the *Birds, Beasts, and Flowers* series and the sequence *Look! We Have Come Through!* This quality remains characteristic of Lawrence: *Etruscan Places*, one of his last writings, has the lucid energy of a series of "acts of attention" which are pure of dogma or self-imposition. Such revelation of quickness in human and nonhuman worlds is *apokalypsis*, in the sense of its being the revelation of that which is immanent but for the most part obscured by received habits of perception.

In Lawrence's work, part of this sense of everchanging life derives from his belief in an intrinsic relatedness between individuals one to another and to the outside world. "If we think about it," he writes,

> we find that our life *consists in* this achieving of a pure relationship between ourselves and the living universe about us. This is how I "save my soul" by accomplishing a pure relationship between me and another person, me and other people, me and a nation, me and a race of men, me and the animals, me and the trees or flowers, me and the earth, me and the skies and sun and stars, me and the moon: an infinity of pure relations, big and little, like the stars of the sky: that makes our eternity, for each one of us, me and the timber I am sawing, the lines of force I follow; me and the dough I knead for bread, me and the very motion with which I write, me and the bit of gold I have got.[17]

A visionary writer such as Lawrence often invites disbelief and hostility. His world is outlandish; his people behave in a way that violates our sympathy or mystifies our understanding; they find themselves in unlikely situations; they seem to think and feel in a violent and unnatural way. The appurtenances of living are made little of: there is no concern for money, only minor interest in the social dilemmas by which we know ourselves and others, nor in the tragic and humorous ironies of creatures for whom "nothing ever runs unmingled."

The author has, on the other hand, an insistent regard for events normally unnoticed; his world is obsessively intense, often with no respite through humor or change of pace. We suffer through passages in which the writer hectors us, insisting that we believe in ideas or events that seem uninteresting and trivial; we are bored and irritated, but he presses on regardless. What is this tyranny, the power of the Ancient Mariner, who must hold the listener through the long nightmare and ecstasy of his tumultuous inner voyage?

It is by his *rhetoric*, it seems, that we know the visionary writer. Many writers seek to "make it new," but for the prophetic artist the vision is so all-encompassing that old forms are inadequate to render its totality. The fermentation of the new wine would burst the old dried wineskins; new hide is needed that will expand to contain the bubbling within.

Lawrence realized the need for new forms adequate to his radical insight. Many statements attest his impatience with the mode expected of him; there is, for instance, the famous letter to Garnett on the "carbon" of character, or the Preface to *New Poems,* or this comment to J.B. Pinker in a letter written in 1915: "Tell Arnold Bennett that all rules of construction hold good only for novels which are copies of other novels. A book which is not a copy of other books has its own construction, and what he calls faults, he being an old imitator, I call characteristics."[18] Again, lambasting the self-conscious modern novel, he demands thoroughgoing change:

> Supposing a bomb were put under the whole scheme of things, what would we be after? What feelings do we want to carry through into the next epoch? What feelings will carry us through? What is the underlying impulse in us that will provide the motive power for a new state of things...?[19]

The visionary writer finds that the new content must be embodied in a new style, and with puzzlement and hostility the reader has to accept this. He is brought into a new world of possibility which he can only test by entering; in the prophet's writing there can be no peering into the work from the vantage point of the known and accepted. The writer demands of the reader at least the imagination of belief: he reverses the old saying so that it becomes "I'll see that when I believe it." In *The Winter's Tale* Paulina thus admonished Leontes, reminding him that if he wished for the miracle to occur—the resurrection of his wife—he must first imagine its possibility, as the entrance into a new order of being. "It is required," she says, "you do awake your faith." Like Leontes, we respond to the lure of an intimation; that which has been experienced as a hunch is now made manifest in the writer as the incarnation of a possibility. Without a response to that lure, without the awakening of faith to enter the charmed world of transformed being, the writing must remain essentially gibberish. (And indeed, when the inspiration fails, as it often does in Lawrence, the writing becomes all manner: tiresome and merely repetitive, rather than incantatory; mumbo-jumbo, pretending to the power of a spell).

Part of our resistance to visionary writing is our resistance to the temporal transvalued, the resistance *of* the temporal to the ingression of that which is more than itself—the "eternal," the "spiritual." The visionary traffics with two worlds: one, "the visible, material, 'real' world"—in Joyce Carol Oates's description—,"the other a world no less real, but not physically demonstrable."[20] The visionary, says Northrop Frye, "creates or dwells in a higher spiritual world in which the objects of perception in this one have become transfigured and charged with a new intensity of symbolism."[21] When the visionary writer—be it Spenser, Thoreau, Kafka, Yeats, or Lawrence, to name at random—is writing at the top of his bent, the spiritual burns through the temporal, so that whatever the object, at whatever point of contemplation by the reader, the whole vision is there, in that fictive object, at that imaginative moment. For it is precisely that "totality in the particular"—in Kenneth Rexroth's phrase—which the visionary attempts to render: his work is, so to speak, holographic.

The intensity with which the spiritual and temporal worlds come together often creates in such writing an effect of aggressiveness, even of violence. This is seen, for example, in Yeats's "Leda and the Swan." Did Leda, Yeats speculates, understand—in fact, bring into being—at Helen's conception the events which Zeus knew would unfold thereafter? "Did she put on his knowledge with his power / Before the indifferent beak could let her drop?" This question is germane, too, for the reader overtaken by the power of visionary rhetoric. Reading a visionary writer becomes an apocalyptic act, for visionary writing is essentially apocalyptic; the vision is total, not just a modification of sensibility but the destruction and remaking of an epistemology.

If eternity is in love with the productions of time, it can only be through the temporal that the visionary writer understands and expresses himself. Being artist rather than mystic, he is intent to explore the interdependence of temporal and spiritual; and like Wallace Stevens, as a modern writer he is aware that such exploration must be an "act of finding what will suffice." He has no traditional prism of belief, valuing the different wavelengths of reality, by which he may organize his vision. Instead, structure must be found within the writer's characteristic rhetoric: Blake's system of giant forms, Yeats's structure of mask and gyre and wheel, Wordsworth's use of the epic form to express the new magnitude of the individual's quest, Thoreau's ironic "cosmic wordplay," Kafka's dream world of incomprehensible lucidity. These are the means by which the writer articulates a vision of the "one fire" (in Lawrence's phrase) burning within temporal reality.

One of the models most consistently used by Lawrence for the structuring of vision was that of apocalypse—the creation of scenes which bring into being "new heaven and earth." As Yeats found in creating the system which he outlined in *A Vision,* such structures make it possible to hold in one context the temporal and the eternal, "reality and justice."[22] Apocalyptic imagery and the narrative of apocalypse gave Lawrence an imaginative form within which he could express his belief in the interfusion of spiritual and temporal, his radical understanding of the Divine.

The Almighty has shifted His throne, and we've got to find a new road. Therefore we've got to get off the old road. You can't stay on the old road, and find a new road. We've got to find our way to God. From time to time Man wakes up and realizes that the Lord Almighty has made a great removal, and passed over the known horizon. Then starts the frenzy, the howling, the despair. Much better listen to the dark hound of heaven, and start off into the dark of the unknown, in search.[23]

2

The Rainbow: Covenant of Renewal

But as the days of Noe were, so shall also the coming of the Son of man be. For as in the days that were before the flood they were eating and drinking, marrying and giving in marriage, until the day that Noe entered into the ark, and knew not until the flood came, and took them all away; so shall also the coming of the Son of man be.

(Matthew 24: 37-39)

The image of the Flood, a prefiguring of catastrophic apocalypse, occurs in several forms in *The Rainbow,* from Tom Brangwen's death by drowning to the inner deluge suffered by various of the characters in the novel.

Though primarily concerned with the destiny of individuals, the novel records too the passing of folkways as they move into dissolution. Marsh Farm, the center of the old life, is flooded by the breaking of an embankment that connects the newly opened collieries, and Tom Brangwen, the last exemplar of the peaceful tradition of the farm, is drowned in that flood. In the following chapter, "The Widening Circle," the author moves out from regard of the cherished valley to engage the world of brutalizing industrialism, of unloved work and untimely and distorted growth.

The flood that overwhelms the magnanimous farmer, Tom Brangwen, is a fictionalized version of that catastrophic tide which the author sees as overtaking the England of his remembered childhood; and his dread will soon be augmented by the floodwave of the Great War. He speaks of this destructive tide in a long nostalgic letter to Lady Ottoline Morrell, describing with sad affection her beautiful Tudor house, Garsington Manor, with its "perfect old intervention of fitted stone," memorial of a life now in retreat; the ancient shade trees in the park; the terraced ornamental ponds; the manor farm where work is seemly and satisfying; the vistas beyond of hedgerow and ploughland—a landscape of time-honored cultivation and order.

It is the vision of a drowning man, the vision of all that I am, all I have become, and ceased to be. It is me, generations and generations of me, every complex, gleaming fibre of me, every lucid pang of my coming into being. And oh, my God, I cannot bear it. For it is not this me who am drowning swiftly under this last wave of time, this bursten flood. . . .[1]

Lawrence's visit to Garsington in the autumn of 1915 crystallized his sense of impending doom.

> When I drive across this country, with autumn falling and rustling to pieces, I am so sad, for my country, for this great wave of civilisation, 2000 years, which is now collapsing, that it is hard to live. So much beauty and pathos of old things passing away and no new things coming: . . . For the winter stretches ahead, where all vision is lost and all memory dies out.[2]

During the early war years he tried to rally his friends to escape the deluge, to ride out the inundation of the old world through escape to Florida; or, failing that, to Cornwall—to a new world where, with his wife and friends, he would live in natural order "blithely by a big river, where there are fish, and in the forest behind wild turkeys and quails; there we [would] make songs and poems and stories and dramas, in a Vale of Avalon, in the Hesperides, among the Loves."[3]

In the plot of *The Rainbow*, the flood marks the passing of a culture, the demise of a beloved but superseded England, as Lawrence was to mourn it in letters to friends beginning the following year. By that time his mood had become even more gloomy, and he sounded more unsure of the flood's eventual abatement. In *The Rainbow*, however, a sense of covenant remains strong, and it speaks to the generational structure of the novel. In the Genesis account of the Deluge, after disaster regeneration is promised. "While the earth remaineth, seedtime and harvest, and cold and heat, and summer and winter, and day and night shall not cease" (Genesis 8:22).

So the novel, though looking always to the possibilities of a future, is replete with history, and with the steadiness of continuing growth and decay: with physical birth, growing, mating, aging; with the seeding and harvesting of crops, the care of livestock and the rearing of children. In one of the finest scenes—that in which Tom tries to calm his frenzied stepchild as his wife cries in labor—the forces of generation gather in collision and harmony. The moaning of the woman in labor rends Tom as he sits downstairs away from and yet a part of Lydia's ordeal. His vagrant mind remembers

> the sound of owls that used to fly round the farmstead when he was a boy. He was back in his youth, a boy, haunted by the sound of the owls, waking up his brother to speak to him. And his mind drifted away to the birds, their solemn, dignified faces, their flight so soft and broad-winged. And then to the birds his brother had shot, fluffy, dust-coloured, dead heaps of softness with faces absurdly asleep. It was a queer thing, a dead owl.[4]

The child, Anna, fearful for her mother's safety, refuses to let Tilly put her to bed, and begins to cry frantically, increasing Tilly's alarm and Tom's anxiety. The child in despair, the servant solicitous and ineffectual, the husband numbed in anguish as wife and stepchild suffer—the scene is wonderfully rendered, as is its resolution: "We'll go an' supper-up the beast." Detail by detail, a new world of tranquility is brought into being as Tom carries the child on his arm back and forth among the cows. Anna gradually relaxes in the unhurried and peaceful atmosphere of the barn.

The covenant of renewal is apparent everywhere in the novel's primarily pastoral setting; but the sign of the covenant, the rainbow, is particularly an image of psychic regeneration in the novel. In the final scene, Ursula, pondering the fate of the colliers, finds hope in the persistent effort of the human being toward self-renewal.

> She knew that the sordid people who crept hard-scaled and separate on the face of the world's corruption were living still,... that they would cast off their horny covering of disintegration, that new, lean, naked bodies would issue to a new germination, to a new growth, rising to the light and the wind and the clean rain of heaven (*Rainbow*, p. 495).

So had the author described the farmers' certainty of physical renewal in the opening chapter, with its verbal echoes of the Genesis covenant. In the course of the novel, unspoken confidence in the continuance and worth of the orderly processes of life becomes conscious, is questioned, lost, and sought for in new circumstances, a new time. It is finally discovered, at least in promise, as Ursula asserts her trust in renewal as an inextinguishable human characteristic, a promise that will be kept: "The rainbow was arched in their blood and would quiver to life in their spirit" (*Rainbow*, p. 495).

In his foreword to *Women in Love,* Lawrence describes the effort of self-understanding through the image of a growing plant:

> Man struggles with his unborn needs and fulfillment. New unfoldings struggle up in torment in him, as buds struggle forth from the midst of a plant. Any man of real individuality tries to know and to understand what is happening, even in himself, as he goes along.[5]

New germination, or budding, like the rainbow's promise of continuance, is an image employed several times in *The Rainbow,* suggesting not only the natural, spontaneous quality of self-renewal, but the death that precedes it.[6] "Except a corn of wheat fall into the ground and die, it abideth alone: but if it die, it bringeth forth much fruit" (John 12:24). Needing sun and rain for growth, the seed is an image that also recalls the nature of covenant. "The strength and patient effort of the new germination" (*Rainbow*, p. 494) in inner or outer growth cannot be accomplished through the isolated effort of the aspirant.

The image of the germinating seed, then, is a figure parallel in effect to that of the Genesis flood: in both, destruction must precede new growth, and in both renewal takes place as a result of a covenant, in that more than the organism itself is responsible for its continuance. Though the other agencies may be inscrutable or unregarded, there is a sense of the bargain kept: the rain will fall, the seasons will come and go in due order.

In *The Rainbow* Lawrence traces the history of three Brangwen generations, but devotes the greatest amount of attention to the latest representative of the family, Ursula, whose early life illustrates Lawrence's conviction that within a person "new unfoldings struggle up in torment—as buds struggle forth from the midst of a plant." Each of the Brangwens struggles to "come to be" to the fullest extent possible within the limitations of his or her own history, parentage, and possible range of experience." But Ursula most completely embodies the passage from "blood intimacy" to consciousness. Her life stands behind the statement that "the rainbow was arched in their blood and would quiver to life in their spirit." She lives in the novel with the magnitude, therefore, of the exemplary hero who suffers in the body the trials of his people—in this case in order to find out what her culture really wants for itself and what will be the form of the new germination.[7]

Ursula's role as pilgrim, seeker, and spiritual hunter is made clear within a short episode in which she contemplates marriage with Anthony Schofield, the brother of her friend Maggie. Anthony is much like the early Brangwens; he is a gardener and a Pan-like figure who has instinctive understanding of his work. Ursula is greatly attracted to him.

> She went down with him into the warmish cellar, where already in the darkness the little yellow knobs of rhubarb were coming. He held the lantern down to the dark earth. She saw the tiny knob-end of the rhubarb thrusting upwards upon the thick red stem, thrusting itself like a knob of flame through the soft soil. His face was turned up to her, the light glittered on his eyes and his teeth as he laughed, with a faint musical neigh (*Rainbow,* p. 414).

He extinguishes her mind, but physically she is mesmerized, and all but accepts his proposal of marriage. "What more does one want," Ursula says, "than to live in this beautiful place, and make things grow in your garden. It is like the garden of Eden" (*Rainbow,* p. 416). But the moon rises at sunset, strange and yellow above the snow, and Ursula realizes that Anthony is unaware of the beauty of the scene although he is so much a part of it. Her apperception divides them absolutely, for, as she reflects later, "she was a traveler, she was a traveler on the face of the earth, and he was an isolated creature living in the fulfillment of his own senses" (*Rainbow,* p. 417).

She sees Schofield much as Lawrence saw the happy physical being of the South Sea islander, in writing about Melville's *Typee,* the island paradise of the Marquesans: "he is centuries and centuries behind us in the life struggle, the consciousness-struggle, the struggle of the soul into fullness." For, he goes on, "Life is never a thing of continuous bliss. There is no paradise. Fight and laugh and feel bitter and feel bliss: and fight again. Fight, fight. That is life."[8]

Such is the struggle in *The Rainbow* as the characters fight to wake from their "generative daze"; and as the plot develops, in a series of "birthings," each generation grows to a greater degree of self-awareness and freedom of action.

And yet the image of the unknowing creature living from his senses continues to lure the writer. Throughout Lawrence's work from *The White Peacock* to *Lady Chatterley's Lover* runs a dialectical argument between the man who is perfectly in accord with the organic processes of death and renewal, living without introspection or sense of a "beyond," and the one who must consciously know himself and the world as a process of growth and destruction. This argument reflects both Lawrence's understanding from boyhood of the life of his relatives and associates, the instinctual miners, and the very different intellectual life of the writer that was his own chosen life. The fictional dialectic begins in Lawrence's first novel, where it forms one of the primary themes of the book.

The setting of *The White Peacock* is much like that of the early part of *The Rainbow*—the Marsh Farm and Cossethay episodes. The narrator's birthplace, where most of the action takes place, is a peaceful valley in which the encroachment of industrial life seems hardly to touch the life or landscape of the characters. In fact, although the scene is drawn from the countryside around Eastwood, as is that of *Sons of Lovers,* in *The White Peacock* Lawrence omitted the mines that form so important a part of the life of the later novel, in order to provide a more consistently pastoral atmosphere.

Yet the narrator, like Melville among the Typees, is restless in his Edenlike home, which he finds he must leave, though his subsequent quest appears extremely indeterminate and he envies his friend Emily's satisfaction in living the even round of farming tasks. He criticizes George, Emily's brother, for accepting such a life, unquestioned, its peace unearned. "Your life," he tells him at the beginning of the novel, "is nothing else but a doss."[9] The development of the plot is the slow wakening of George to a life of ideas, values, and friendships in a world beyond his bucolic torpor. Yet this knowledge destroys him; for, half awake, he is unable fully to comprehend and to take hold of that world he is led to imagine, particularly as it is embodied in Lettie, whom he loves. Instead, losing Lettie to an educated rival, he makes a desperate marriage and sinks gradually into alcoholism. On the other hand, Annable, the gamekeeper, embodies the vividness of the robust physical life that was originally George's and which the author presents as a way of being opposed, as a more attractive reality, to that of the enervated Leslie, Lettie's cultured suitor.

Yet the rifts and misgivings between and within the characters are subsumed within a lyrical plot that is essentially a dialogue between the narrator and his loved paradise, the valley of Nethermere. The novel was to be, as Lawrence described its conception to Jessie Chambers, the story of the developing relationship between two couples, in the manner of George Eliot.

But, unlike Eliot, who found the moral dilemmas of her characters to be deserving of intense scrutiny, in Lawrence's novel the canvas becomes a landscape with figures.[10] As I have pointed out, there are conflicts within and between the characters which in later fiction Lawrence would develop vigorously. The participants suffer further loss and frustration: the death of the father, the violent death of Annable, George's pitiful degradation, and Lettie's increasingly lonely life in an unsatisfying marriage. Yet none of these experiences of deprivation is felt with a reality as clearly present to the writer as is that of the landscape itself. Even the narrator's last dialogue with his sick friend is somewhat decorative, life being in the setting rather than the human situation.

> Across the empty cornfield the partridges were running. We walked through the September haze slowly, because he was feeble on his legs. As he became tired he ceased to talk. We leaned for some time on a gate, in the brief glow of the transient afternoon, and he was stupid again. He did not notice the brown haste of the partridges, he did not care to share with me the handful of ripe blackberries, and when I pulled the bryony ropes off the hedges, and held the great knots of red and green berries in my hand, he glanced at them without interest or appreciation.
> "Poison-berries, aren't they?" he said dully.
> Like a tree that is falling, going soft and pale and rotten, clammy with small fungi, he stood leaning against the gate, while the dim afternoon drifted with a flow of thick sweet sunshine past him, not touching him (*White Peacock*, pp. 366-67).

More strongly realized than the loss of his friend is the loss of the narrator's birthplace.

> Since I left the valley of home I have not much feared any other loss. The hills of Nethermere had been my walls, and the sky of Nethermere my roof overhead. It seemed almost as if, at home, I might lift my hand to the ceiling of the valley, and touch my own beloved sky, whose familiar clouds came again and again to visit me, whose stars were constant to me, born when I was born, whose sun had been all my father to me. But now the skies were strange over my head, and Orion walked past me unnoticing, he who night after night had stood over the woods to spend with me a wonderful hour (*White Peacock*, pp. 298-99).

For this is where the author's real involvement lies. His affections, like those of Cyril his narrator, are rooted in Nethermere, the fictionalized environs of Felley Mill, a countryside which he evokes with subtlety and intimacy, attentive to its moods, as a lover reluctant to leave. The novel bears the marks of the homesickness described by Cyril, Lawrence's own when he wrote, in "exile" in Croydon, of the countryside of his strongest affections. Much later, a year before his death, he wrote in a letter to J.D. Chambers, Jessie's brother:

> I shall never forget the Haggs—I loved it so. I loved to come to you all, it really was a new life began in me there. The water-pippin by the door—those maiden-blush roses that Flower would lean over and eat and trip floundering round. —And stewed figs for tea in winter, and

in August green stewed apples. Do you still have them? Tell your mother I never forgot, no matter where life carries us.... Whatever else I am, I am somewhere still the same Bert who rushed with such joy to the Haggs.[11]

Not even the religious awe he experienced in discovering the American Southwest penetrated Lawrence's inner landscape as deeply as the Nottingham-Derby border of his childhood, when "it was still the old England of the forest and agricultural past; there were no motor-cars, the mines were, in a sense, an accident in the landscape, and Robin Hood and his merry men were not very far away."[12]

The White Peacock represents a partial reality. Cyril, who is identified with the questing consciousness of the writer, remains an indeterminate being functioning as the sensitive receptor of the moods and changes of the seasonal cycle of the valley, moved to vague longings by the observation of cloud masses and uneasy with the falling of the leaves. Only rarely—in encounters between Lettie and George—does the inner life between and within persons possess any of the vibrancy of Lawrence's subsequent work; that close tracking of human feeling which is characteristic of *The Rainbow* is only intimated in *The White Peacock*.

In *The Rainbow*, pastoral is transformed by the writer's determination to pay close attention to the real conflicts and meetings in relationship—within the self, between persons, and with the individual in connection with his experience beyond the personal. In short, he deals in *The Rainbow* with aspects of covenant.

"I shall always be a priest of love," wrote Lawrence to Mrs. S.A. Hopkin in December 1912. In a letter to Edward Garnett in April 1913, apropos of "The Sisters," he writes that the most important theme for the novelist of the day is exploration of the relationship between men and women. "It is *the* problem of today, the establishment of a new relation, or the re-adjustment of the old one between men and women."[13] Lawrence had, of course, been made vividly—indeed cataclysmically—aware of "the establishment of a new relation" between men and women by recent events in his own life. In April 1912 he met Frieda Weekley and eloped with her to London and Germany, where they spent the summer fighting for a measure of peace together.

Lawrence discusses the fictional establishment of this new relation between persons also in a celebrated letter to Edward Garnett in which he claims that he deals with the "carbon" of relationship rather than its derivatives, with the "elemental" conflict and attraction which form the unmined strata of human meetings. These strata, he believed, run deeper and contain truer ore than that hitherto brought to the surface by writers of fiction.[14]

Lawrence therefore needed new analogies with which to articulate such relationships. One such is an ancient model of experience, thus described in "The Reality of Peace":

Does any story of martyrdom affect us like the story of the conversion of Paul? In an age of barrenness, where people glibly talk of epilepsy on the road to Damascus, we shy off from the history, we hold back from realizing what is told. We dare not know. We dare to gloat on the crucifixion, but we dare not face the mortal fact of the conversion from the accepted world, to the new world which was not yet conceived, that took place in the soul of St. Paul on the road to Damascus.[15]

For three days and nights after his conversion St. Paul was blind within the light; only later did he begin to understand mentally what he had already accepted, the meaning of his vision. At first, he was converted from the "accepted world" to a transfigured world which was "not yet conceived." So Lawrence speaks of a man's courage "to yield himself to the unknown that should make him new and vivid, to yield himself deliberately in faith."[16]

In *The Rainbow* conversion is a radical model of decision. The narrative develops as a series of psychic conflagrations and renewals which occur cataclysmically, throwing into new alignment the whole being of the character involved, altering not only a decision on this or that matter, but more fundamentally his understanding of the world.

I can most clearly illustrate such dynamics of conversion by describing first the action of a story written just a year and a half after Lawrence finished *The Rainbow:* "The Horse Dealer's Daughter"; for in this story the dramatic action is described with the succinctness necessary to its short story form.

The action takes place in a drab mining town on a damp winter's day; those involved, a young doctor and the horse dealer's adult sons and daughter, are characters presented as at a low ebb of vitality; there is an atmosphere, marvelously presented, of the most grinding dreariness. The story describes the suicide attempt of Mabel, the daughter who, desperate at the impasse brought about by her family's hopeless financial state, walks into the lake near her home. She is rescued by the young doctor, who—having more or less accidentally witnessed the scene—drags her from the pond, resuscitates her, carries her home, and wraps her, naked, in dry blankets. Recovering consciousness and learning her situation, Mabel asks, "Do you love me, then?" The question is apparently unprepared. Scarcely more than acquaintances, the two seem to have little awareness of each other, much less love. However, the story illustrates a different kind of meeting, one discovered through what Anaïs Nin calls "interlinear communication" between persons, the "constant effort to make conscious and articulate the silent, subconscious communications between human beings."[17]

Earlier, in Mabel's kitchen, the young doctor had found himself drawn to her impassivity, her self-contained silence, and "steady, dangerous eyes, that always made him uncomfortable, unsettling his superficial ease."[18] He is a nervous man who, hating the dreary laborious round of duties in the sordid mining town, is yet stimulated by the working people, with their very different emotional life. Mabel also lives a divided life, or, more accurately, the life of a somnambulist. Since the death of her mother she has cherished her memory, idealizing her and finding that "the life she followed here in the world was far less real than the world of death she inherited from her mother" ("Horse Dealer's Daughter," p. 448). The family's financial collapse, a disaster for the brothers, seems to her a kind of triumph, drawing her closer to her dead mother.

A contact has already been established, therefore, between the two when the doctor notices Mabel tending her mother's grave, away as if in another world, and he is touched by the breath of the unknown. No words are exchanged, but recognition passes between them, "each feeling in some way found out by the other." The alien presence of the woman, the sense of an unknown entity that yet speaks to his own being, restores his vitality. "He had been feeling weak and done before. Now the life came back to him, he felt delivered from his own fretted daily self" ("Horse Dealer's Daughter," p. 448). A change has come upon him, unwilled, even in a sense unwanted, yet it seems to be an authentic message from his inner self. The exchange has been wordless, nor does he subsequently think about his encounter as he finishes his duties and goes on his professional rounds. However, at that "carbon" level of his being his life has radically changed, the change realizing itself in a later confession of love that surprises him as much as it does Mabel. It is with seeming indifference that he rescues her from the pond, figuratively and also literally reaching through death to bring her to the upper world, since he himself all but drowns, for an instant, in the dark water. She, for her part, so near the annihilation of herself, in the deathly motion to be with the mother she had visited in the underworld of life-in-death, draws the doctor after her so that he himself visits Hades to try for her return.

Thus the scene of their declaration of mutual love is in fact fully prepared, but all in an almost wordless, subliminal manner, so that, when it comes, it is with shocking and painful realization. The doctor resists the contact, yet recognizes its supremacy; he is tormented by his admission of love.

> With an inward groan he gave way, and let his heart yield towards her. A sudden gentle smile came on his face. And her eyes, which never left his face, slowly, slowly filled with tears....
> ... "You love me?" she said, rather faltering.
> "Yes." The word cost him a painful effort. Not because it wasn't true. But because it was too newly true, the *saying* seemed to tear open again his newly-torn heart. And he hardly wanted it to be true, even now.... He never intended to love her. But now it was over. He had crossed over the gulf to her, and all that he had left behind had shriveled and become void ("Horse Dealer's Daughter," pp. 454-55).

The scene is painful in its close tracking from the doctor's point of view of confused and violent feelings. It is grotesque in that an impassioned and romantic moment is thrust upon a setting which is, if not sordid, at best drearily humdrum. Yet beyond this, the writer finds a grim beauty in the doctor's acknowledgment of his discovery of love for the woman. His feeling for her had come unwilled, but he realizes that it is authentic; and he knows, now, as his body had known at the graveyard, that this contact between them has changed his life.

In contrast, consider a similar scene in Hardy's *Far from the Madding Crowd,* a novel which Lawrence knew well. The episode occurs early in the relationship between Gabriel and Bathsheba, and from his rather cumbrous introduction we understand that Hardy intends this to be an important episode in their developing intimacy.

We have learned that Gabriel is intrigued by the arrival in the neighborhood of the attractive and flirtatious Bathsheba. One night, up with his ewes at lambing time, Gabriel falls asleep in his unventilated hut. Rescued in the nick of time by Bathsheba, he recovers consciousness to find himself in her lap. Though moved by Gabriel's near death, both he and she are presented as acting within the bonds and conventions of their social and sexual situation; or rather, their heightened emotional state is played off by the author *against* the roles within their convention: Gabriel decorously earnest, Bathsheba somewhat flirtatious, each according to the characteristics established for them in earlier episodes. The result of the incident is that Gabriel finds himself infatuated by Bathsheba, yet none of this passion is explored as process within the scene. Hardy's mode is that of comedy in setting up established character against an unsettling situation.

Lawrence is less interested—as he said to Garnett—in the former proprieties of narrative discourse: in reliance on action within an understood stable social context or on steady attention to the likelihood of outer events as appropriate to realistic narrative. Rather, he is intent, if need be, on violating these accepted limits in order to create a symbolic pattern which articulates a different morality, one more truly intrinsic, in his view, to human relationships, from which manners and morals themselves derive. His fictional patterns, therefore, will "fall into the form of some other rhythmic form, as when one draws a fiddle-bow across a fine tray delicately sanded, the sand takes lines unknown."[19]

One analogy Lawrence finds for this other rhythmic form is, as I have said, conversion. This involves cataclysmic destruction of a former way of seeing and its replacement by a new understanding, not at first rationally understood, a luminous experience of the unknown. It is this unknown in the woman to which the doctor responds in "The Horse Dealer's Daughter"; and, as in St. Paul's conversion, the birth of love in the story is sudden, subverting the doctor's whole being as he had perceived it. The event is not understood by him, yet is perfectly clear in another sense. He is blind within the light. Indeed the whole scene is described through images of light and fire, images of transfiguration, which is another figure of conversion. Ferguson perceives Mabel thus transformed: "In view of the delicate flame which seemed to come from her face like a light, he was powerless" ("Horse Dealer's Daughter," p. 453). Such a radical transformation of modality is the result of a radical change in perception.

When Tom Brangwen first meets his future wife, it is with the same sudden certainty of encounter and the same sense of being "blind within the light," of having made a decision, yet mentally being far behind that decision; it is a leap into the unknown, made on other than rational grounds. Thus, passing on the road one day a stranger to the community, he notices her absent manner: "It was her curious, absorbed, flitting motion, as if she were passing unseen by everybody, that first arrested him" (*Rainbow*, p. 23). Then he notices her features: "He saw her face clearly, as if by a light in the air."

> "That's her," he said involuntarily. As the cart passed by, splashing through the thin mud, she stood back against the bank. Then, as he walked still beside his britching horse, his eyes met hers. He looked quickly away, pressing back his head, a pain of joy running through him. He could not bear to think of anything.

As she passes, his world is overturned.

> He felt as if he were walking again in a far world, not Cossethay, a far world, the fragile reality. He went on, quiet, suspended, rarefied. . . . He moved within the knowledge of her, in the world that was beyond reality (*Rainbow*, p. 24).

It would seem that the moment of transformation is utterly unprepared; but again we realize that earlier scenes have enacted a wordless gestation of intent. Tom is frustrated, suffering a sense of impasse in his life. He is further unsettled after an earlier meeting with a foreigner who becomes in his fantasy the image of the archaic power of a knowledge beyond him, suave and sensual, for "amidst this subtle intimacy was always the satisfaction of a voluptuous woman" (*Rainbow*, p. 20). He is ready for his meeting with Lydia, though he does not himself know it consciously. It is only, therefore, the *form* of its fulfillment that is hidden from him.

He learns from Tilly of Lydia's Polish history, glad of her strangeness and unthinkingly sure of her, in connection with himself.

> A swift change had taken place on the earth for him, as if a new creation were fulfilled, in which he had real existence. Things had all been stark, barren, mere nullities before. Now they were actualities that he could handle (*Rainbow*, p. 26).

Curiously the "unreal" world of his perception of their relationship has become for him the ground of a greater sense of reality.

Some while later Lydia comes to Marsh Farm to borrow a pound of butter. The meeting between Tom and Lydia is awkward, each discovering the other through unconscious gesture, the words passing between them being merely the excuse, the hardly understood forms of social convention making the meeting possible, yet having little to do with it. Each is attracted by the difference of manner of the other; he by her withdrawn self-possession, she by a kind of large easiness, freshness, and confidence. Characteristically the narrator moves back and forth between the two experiencing consciousnesses, closely following the feelings of each. Each is drawn to the inner presence of the other; and when she leaves, Brangwen is profoundly moved by the casual event: "In his breast or in his bowels, somewhere in his body, there had started another activity." His being is transformed. "It was as if a strong light were burning there, and he was blind within it, unable to know anything, except that this transfiguration burned between him and her, connecting them, like a secret power" (*Rainbow*, p. 33).

Still he does not understand rationally what has evolved within him. Thus he is blind; but he is also filled with non-rational insight, irradiated with certain knowledge, as was St. Paul on the road to Damascus. After this event he finds himself "drifting, quiescent, in a state of metamorphosis," submissive to "that which was happening to him, letting go his will, suffering the loss of himself, dormant always on the brink of ecstasy, like a creature evolving to a new birth" (*Rainbow*, pp. 33-34). And so the new life that comes upon him unwilled also brings him closer to himself. It fulfills his own inner, unformed aspirations.

There is an impersonal quality to the meeting of Tom and Lydia, as if a power distinct from themselves passes through them at such a moment. Although Lawrence uses biblical images of transfiguration, conversion, deluge, and resurrection in *The Rainbow*, he does not commit himself to a Christian point of view.[20] Yet he insists on some non-human power, if not directing human energies, at least immanent in these energies.

> But during the long February nights with the ewes in labour, looking out from the shelter into the flashing stars, he knew he did not belong to himself. He must admit that he was only fragmentary, something incomplete and subject. There were the stars in the dark heaven travelling, the whole host passing by on some eternal voyage. So he sat small and submissive to the greater ordering (*Rainbow*, p. 35).

Lawrence writes to Campbell in September, 1914:

> We want to realize the tremendous *non-human* quality of life—it is wonderful. It is not the emotions, nor the personal feelings and attachments, that matter. These are all only expressive, and expression has become mechanical. Behind in all are the tremendous unknown forces of life, coming unseen and unperceived as out of the desert to the Egyptians, and driving us, forcing us, destroying us if we do not submit to be swept away."[21]

So it is that Brangwen understands his life with Lydia, as if both participate in a greater ordering. The sense of an unspoken convenant persists in the exploring of connection between individuals. Throughout *The Rainbow* the writer declines to name or discuss such covenant, while everywhere testifying to its reality.[22]

It is not only the meeting of Tom and Lydia that is described in terms of cataclysm as the opening of perception to a new reality. Will and Anna meet in similar clash of attraction, as they surprise themselves by the discovery of passion.

> And he dared not think of her face, of her eyes which shone, and of her strange, transfigured face. The hand of the Hidden Almighty, burning bright, had thrust out of the darkness and gripped him. He went on subject and in fear, his heart gripped and burning from the touch (*Rainbow*, p. 115).

Lawrence sees their encounter as the apocalyptic Day of the Lord in which "the heavens shall pass away with a great noise and the elements shall melt with fervent heat" (II Peter 3:10). This is true not only of their early meetings but also of the passionate duel that ensues after their marriage. "Everything glowed intensely about them, the world had put off its clothes and was awful, with new, primal nakedness" (*Rainbow*, p. 165).

The sudden breaking up of an old way of seeing to allow entry of the new reality—the experience of conversion—this is in *The Rainbow* a model of the way in which two individuals come to understand one another.[23]

There is in the novel, however, a way other than that of the analogy of apocalyptic conversion by which a passionate meeting between individuals is articulated. In many episodes the characters realize their sense of each other through participation in an event that includes but is not limited to themselves; in which the revelation, the understanding, is of a degree of relationship that is not confined to the human participants, but embraces the non-human world as well. As an example, I should like to look at a scene in *The White Peacock* and one in *The Rainbow*, both of which contain a proposal of marriage.

Lettie's ill-starred acceptance of Leslie Tempest is set in the context of a dismally wet afternoon in which the landscape seems to echo the spiritless melancholy which is her mood in contemplating the forthcoming engagement. A crow flops across the garden, ill-omened; the leaves lie fallen and sodden; the wind drives through sullen trees. The scene is effective in a Tennysonian way, reflecting the dreary and resigned mood of the watchers.

Tom Brangwen walks to his intended wife's home on an evening much like this, the wind whipping the trees at twilight; but the scene vibrates with a life that is not reflected from the human participants. Emotionally wrought up by his intention, he knows that a certain evening is the time to ask Lydia to marry him. Again the moment "comes upon" him: "One evening in March, when the wind was roaring outside, came the moment to ask her" (*Rainbow*, p. 36). Season and wind have apparently causal weight, as entering into his decision, parallel to but not derivative from Tom's state of mind. As he walks to the vicarage he is aware, as is the participant reader, of a correspondence between his inner state and the life of his surroundings. "The wind was roaring in the apple trees, the yellow flowers swayed violently up and down, he heard even the fine whisper of their spears as he stooped to break the flattened, brittle stems of the flowers" (*Rainbow*, p. 37). The writer is not so much intent on creating analogies between inner and outer worlds as on capturing the whole scene as an interplay of forceful energies, individual each to itself but partaking of a central power. The roaring wind, the brittle pale flowers, the desiring man—all are equally participant in a burning field of energy, the immanent coming-to-be of living phenomena. Lawrence reveals an event in which Tom's feeling for Lydia is in some way influenced by twilight, wind, appletree, and daffodil, as are they in their turn modified by Tom in his anticipated meeting with Lydia.[24]

In this scene, as in other such moments in the novel, the characters in a state of heightened emotion find—and draw the reader into—a world transfigured, vibrantly alive and connected one part with another. Such life and such correspondence Lawrence finds to be everywhere immanent, yet it needs the emotional excitement of an unusual state of mind—such as Tom's in this scene—to recover awareness of its reality. This is revelation, in the sense of *apokalypsis,* the unveiling, a discovery of the new world within the old through a radical change of perception: "There is another world," exclaims Paul Éluard, "and it is this one!"[25]

Such moments are to be of the greatest importance to theme and structure in *Women in Love;* in *The Rainbow,* plot as such is less dependent on this kind of revelation, although a number of important decisions are arrived at through such scenes.

The celebrated episode in which Will and Anna gather sheaves together results in Will's unthought declaration: "We'll get married, Anna"; but the resolve has been unconsciously formed in the course of the ritual marriage which they have just celebrated, when, as the author says, "something fixed in him for ever." Anna was, he realized, his wife. They move back and forth in the field pairing the ripe sheaves beneath an incandescent moon whose rhythms form a counterpart to the ebb and flow of the tide of the lovers' movement up and down the dusky meadow. They are enfolded within an erotic event expressed through ancient images of fertility: dew-drenched grain, moonlight, the erotic dance-like meeting and passing of the lovers. The darkness of sexual confrontation between the two, as later described in the novel, is connected with the dark night, with the darkness within Anna herself; but darkness, moon, corn, girl and man—all are equally participant. This is no anthropomorphic creation of the world as subsumed under man's domination. The symbols by which we understand the lovers' meeting are as authentic and vital as the movements of consciousness that are dramatized through them. It is within this process that Anna and Will discover further their commitment to each other; it is as well the *means* by which such commitment is revealed to them and articulated as narrative by the author. In the same way Tom had found himself caught up in an event that transcended his personal courtship; his feelings revealed the correspondences between himself and his world through which he understood himself, Lydia, and his marriage.

In contrast to this experience of the moon in her procreative aspect, there are scenes in which Ursula is identified with the destructive forces of the moon, when, full of corrosive will, she destroys her lover Skrebensky. These too are turning points, dramatic revelations of what both had known within themselves to be the reality of their passion of conflict. Thus at the wedding of her cousin, Ursula realizes that she can go no further with Skrebensky, that their wills are irrevocably opposed. As they kiss, her strength of will, passionately bent on overcoming him, annihilates Skrebensky, so that he acknowledges himself defeated, he possessing a less powerful will than Ursula. Yet the force of the scene, the force by which they know this to be a turning point, lies in the total event. As with Anna and Will's sheaf gathering, a ritual atmosphere is established within the scene through mimesis of the sinuous motion of the firelit dance.

> There was a wonderful rocking of the darkness, slowly, a great, slow swinging of the whole night, with the music playing lightly on the surface, making the strange, ecstatic, rippling on the surface of the dance, but underneath only one great flood heaving slowly backwards to the verge of oblivion, slowly forward to the other verge, the heart sweeping along each time, and tightening with anguish as the limit was reached, and the movement, at crises, turned and swept back (*Rainbow*, pp. 316-17).

Ursula is suddenly aware of the moon's rising, a powerful presence, numinous and baleful: "And she danced on and on with Skrebensky, while the great, white watching continued, balancing all in its revelation" (*Rainbow*, p. 317). Ursula appears to become a creature strangely identified with the moon, the moon no less living than the girl. The event is transformed. Now the human participants act on each other with the motions of natural forces: the corrosion of salt, the weight of gravity, the pull of a lodestone. The world has uncovered a mineral, moon-like reality, brilliant and burning.

> They went towards the stackyard. There he saw, with something like terror, the great new stacks of corn glistening and gleaming transfigured, silvery and present under the night-blue sky, throwing dark, substantial shadows, but themselves majestic and dimly present. She,

like glimmering gossamer, seemed to burn among them, as they rose like cold fires to the silvery-bluish air. All was intangible, a burning of cold, glimmering, whitish-steely fires. He was afraid of the great moon-conflagration of the cornstacks rising above him. His heart grew smaller, it began to fuse like a bead (*Rainbow*, p. 319).

All is found to be elemental: Skrebensky is like soft iron, Ursula's "hands and feet [feel] immensely strong like blades"; she is like pure metal; he the dross, like the other guests an impure admixture.

Thus the decision is found, the revelation accomplished in the *Apokalypsis* which is the character's apprehension—and ours—of the total scene: wedding guests, the great stacks of corn, firelight, the moon's radiance, the two lovers dancing together in elemental opposition.

At such moments as these, the participants apparently slip into a different sense of time; in the fullness of the experience awareness of temporal movement is suspended. Will Brangwen during his honeymoon experiences it thus:

Inside the room was a great steadiness, a core of living eternity. Only far outside, at the rim, went on the noise and the destruction. Here at the centre the great wheel was motionless, centred upon itself. Here was a poised, unflawed stillness that was beyond time, because it remained the same, inexhaustible, unchanging, unexhausted (*Rainbow*, p. 141).

Frank Kermode provides a suggestive way of thinking about such moments in relation to one's customary sense of passing time. Drawing on medieval categories, he describes three kinds of time. The first is time as it relates to matter: that is, time as perishing. Then there is postulated what Boethius called the "nunc stans," the static eternal moment, eternal duration. But Kermode finds in Aquinas a discussion of *angelic* time that opens up a third possibility. Angels are immutable as to substance, says Aquinas: they cannot be destroyed; but through acts of intellect and will they can change. They are therefore neither timebound nor eternal; their mode of time is that third kind of duration, the *aevum*. The term *aevum* can be used to talk about the "soul's attentiveness," the full moment which gives access to the realization of continuity in change. Kermode describes Wordsworth's visionary moments as "the hiding places of power" which are "the agents of time's defeat." Such moments, he goes on, "discovered by involuntary memory, pure of discursive significance like the girl with the pitcher, . . . provide the structure and meaning and pleasure which constitute our deliverance from the long, meaningless attrition of time."[26]

Such is the experience of Will and Anna as they gather corn sheaves under the moonlight, of Ursula with Skrebensky dancing at her cousin's wedding, and again with him on the downs as she watches a perfect dawn begin to break over the land; and in the intensity of its portrayal this richness of experience is the reader's too.

Ursula is described as seeking "a new knowledge of Eternity in the flux of time" (*Rainbow,* p. 492). She can not go back to that unknowing ease with which the Brangwens lived in accord with their environment and their work; yet she seeks a fullness that the Brangwens possessed in that physical life as it is described in the early pages of the novel. For Ursula, Lawrence says:

> the trouble began at evening. Then a yearning for something unknown came over her, a passion for something she knew not what. She would walk the foreshore alone after dusk, expecting, expecting something, as if she had gone to a rendezvous. The salt, bitter passion of the sea, its indifference to the earth, its swinging, definite motion, its strength, its attack, and its salt burning, seemed to provoke her to a pitch of madness, tantalizing her with vast suggestions of fulfillment (*Rainbow,* p. 477).

Her realization of *kairos* must be won from time's destruction.

By the end of the novel Ursula has not found the object of her soul's striving. Yet the book ends with a promise of fulfillment, in Ursula's peace of mind, which has its outer counterpart in the image of the rainbow; and the promise is apparently prepared for by an episode which seemingly has little connection with what has gone before and what follows, that scene in which Ursula is waylaid by a herd of horses. As a result of this encounter it seems that she is able to realize the illusory quality of her commitment to Skrebensky, and to feel within her the beginnings of self-renewal, after the strain of her engagement.

Again this is an episode in which decision is arrived at unconsciously through participation in an event that apparently has no direct bearing on the decision to be made. What part does Ursula's meeting with the horses play in resolving her commitment after all to marry Skrebensky and in providing the climactic moment in her search for selfhood?

Soon after her mistaken agreement to go to India with Skrebensky, the father of her expected child, Ursula wanders out to walk in the rain, passing by the town, through the wood and the common. The scene is drenched with water; the rain is both deluge and lustration. It frees Ursula from that suffocating sense of a wrong direction that had been pressing upon her. Her feeling of constriction has an analogue in her sense of the blighted city, a wet underworld. "Everywhere was drenched wet and deserted, the grimed houses glowed dull red, the butt houses burned scarlet in a gleam of light, under the glistening, blackish purple slates" (*Rainbow,* p. 485). All is beneath the flood; and Ursula's sense is also one of confusion, of drowning. "She was very wet and a long way from home, far enveloped in the rain and the waving landscape. She must beat her way back through all this fluctuation, back to stability and security" (*Rainbow,* p. 486). This is both an inner and an outer state for her.

Yet at the same time she is "glad of the rain's privacy and intimacy"; the rain is a lustration. "She walked the open space where hawthorn trees streamed like hair on the wind and round bushes were presences slowing [*sic*] through the atmosphere. It was very splendid, free and chaotic" (*Rainbow*, p. 486). She is described as a frail bird pitted against the heaviness of the wet tree trunks, hastening between "their grave booming ranks."

A correspondence is established between the outer scene and the girl's inner life, in which each is seen as an alternative mode of being, manifesting a similar reality; discovered in the one case in the dissolving and lustrating sweep of the rain, in the other in the change of heart in the girl, as her burden of commitment to Skrebensky falls away.

Within the wood Ursula stumbles upon a horse herd, which seems to be massed to attack her; she must make her way through the herd to the safety of the fence beyond.

> Horses, always horses! . . . Far back, far back in our dark soul the horse prances. He is a dominant symbol: he gives us lordship: he links us, the first palpable and throbbing link with the ruddy-glowing Almighty of potence: he is the beginning even of our godhead in the flesh. And as a symbol he roams the dark underworld of the soul. He stamps and threshes in the dark fields of your soul and of mine. [27]

And so St. Mawr, the chestnut horse, is an image of splendor: "The red horse is choler: not mere anger, but natural fieriness, what we call passion." [28] As such, he is the dominant image of the novel *St. Mawr*, the node of its power. When he is abandoned to his brood mares, the narrative collapses.

Lawrence, then, finds in the image of the horse a "symbol of surging potency and power of movement, of action, in man." However, it is frustrated force, rather than free energy, that seems to be dominant in our sense of the horse herd in *The Rainbow*—perhaps because they *are* a herd, moving as a unit with a single fixed will. The quality of their presence recalls Ursula's sense of Skrebensky as closed off from himself and from her, rigid in will, passionate, with a limited self-enclosed desire. "The vulnerable variable quick of the man was inaccessible. She knew nothing of it. She could only feel the dark heavy fixity of his animal desire" (*Rainbow*, p. 443).

But perhaps the reader's predominant sense throughout the scene is that of the *movement* rather than of the visual image, which has a hallucinatory, unfocused quality: we are aware of the great haunches, flaring nostrils, the glancing hoofs.

> Large, large seemed the bluish, incandescent flash of the hoof-iron, large as a halo of lightning round the knotted darkness of the flanks. Like circles of lightning came the flash of hoofs from out of the powerful flanks (*Rainbow*, p. 487).

It is presence rather than image that is most clear in the scene—as is often also the case in a dream. [29]

The nightmare quality of the event is prefigured in Ursula's awareness of the great trees looming overhead in the wood, before she meets the horse herd.

> There, the vast booming overhead vibrated down and encircled her, tree-trunks spanned the circle of tremendous sound, myriads of tree-trunks, enormous and streaked black with water, thrust like stanchions upright between the roaring overhead and the sweeping of the circle underfoot. She glided between the tree-trunks, afraid of them. They might turn and shut her in as she went through their martialled silence (*Rainbow*, p. 486).

The horses are like the monsters of nightmare encircling the dreamer, whose escape seems always cut off by their perpetually imminent attack as he tries, though often with a terrifying sense of paralysis, to escape. So Ursula's path through the common to the neighboring field is the dreamer's interminable road, her fear the panic of immovability, of an inescapable hovering annihilation. Yet she comes through her nightmare by relying—as she had in previous crises—on the determinative power of the persistent self. She knows, even as she becomes aware of the herd, that "she would bear the weight steadily and so escape. She would go straight on and on and be gone by" (*Rainbow*, p. 487).

Though, as ever in Lawrence, the participants in the scene each have their own reality, so that the horses are in no way merely "symbolic" of Ursula's state of mind, there is constant slippage or fluidity of reference in the event between inner and outer. Thus, sensing the herd's menace, "she knew the heaviness on her heart. It was the weight of the horses. But she would circumvent them" (*Rainbow*, pp. 486-87). It is impossible not to understand their weight as that inner heaviness, too, of an oppressive commitment to Skrebensky, as the weight of his child, felt as a burden when "gradually the heaviness of her heart pressed and pressed into consciousness" (*Rainbow*, p. 483). The horses are within her, and as she waits for word from Skrebensky she feels "a gathering restiveness, a tumult impending within her" (*Rainbow*, p. 485). This is the inner counterpart of her subsequent encounter. After the event she reenacts the scene at home in different form: that of delirium in which she is once again circumventing the horse herd, now experienced as Skrebensky and as all the forces of massive will, rigidity and coercion in her life.

> She fought and fought and fought all through her illness to be free of him and his world, to put it aside, to put it aside, into its place. Yet ever anew it gained ascendency over her, it laid new hold on her. Oh, the unutterable weariness of her flesh, which she could not cast off, nor yet extricate. If she could but extricate herself, if she could but disengage herself from feeling, from her body, from all the vast encumbrances of the world that was in contact with her, from her father, and her mother, and her lover, and all her acquaintance (*Rainbow*, pp. 491-92).

Then at last she feels herself renewed, dropped like an acorn "lying on the floor of a wood." So had she in her physical being fallen from the oak tree, safe on to the earth, a death preparing for new germination.

> As she sat there, spent, time and the flux of change passed away from her, she lay as if unconscious upon the bed of the stream, like a stone, unconscious, unchanging, unchangeable, whilst everything rolled by in transience, leaving her there, a stone at rest on the bed of the stream, inalterable and passive, sunk to the bottom of all change (*Rainbow*, p. 489).

The awakening finds her, as it had found her parents and grandparents in comparable crises, "blind within the light"; her decision about Skrebensky has been arrived at through non-rational and innerly cataclysmic events: through a psychic death and rebirth. She does not, evidently, analyze her indomitable passage through the horse herd, her persistent fight to regain a sense of reality through the mist and rain; but she has nonetheless been given clarification through the fearful encounter.

> When she woke at last it seemed as if a new day had come on the earth. How long, how long had she fought through the dust and obscurity, for this new dawn? How frail and fine and clear she felt, like the most fragile flower that opens in the end of winter. But the pole of night was turned and the dawn was coming in (*Rainbow*, p. 492).

The reference is to her illness; it also, by implication, includes her struggle with the horses. As in earlier scenes, inner and outer share a single reality of which the constituents, while clear and particular in their own being, yet have—to the author's perception—an interdependence, a homologous relationship one to another, within the event.

So it is that, when Lawrence says of the people of Beldover, sunk as they are in corruption, that yet "the rainbow was arched in their blood," he means that the body contains that same power of joyful renewal which in the physical world of nature appears as the rainbow.

> In the blowing clouds, she saw a band of faint iridescence colouring in faint colours a portion of the hill. And forgetting, startled, she looked for the hovering colour and saw a rainbow forming itself (*Rainbow*, p. 494).

This is a description of the rainbow itself, and also of the forms and rhythms of the delicate, wavering convalescence of the psyche.

The rainbow grows until it dominates the grimy landscape, "making great architecture of light and colour and the space of heaven, its pedestals luminous in the corruption of new houses on the low hill, its arch the top of heaven" (*Rainbow*, p. 494). Ursula sees in the rainbow the sign of the covenant, the promise of new heaven, new earth. Men are creatures who creep "hard scaled on the earth," locked in rigid perception; they are encased in a "horny covering of disintegration"; their activities and artefacts are those of their own narrow fixity. Yet the color, balance, and grace of the rainbow arches within the body, and Ursula sees that it will "quiver to life in their spirit, that they [will] cast off their horny covering of disintegration, that new, clean, naked bodies [will] issue to a new germination, to a new growth, rising to the light and the wind and the clean rain of heaven" (*Rainbow,* p. 495). There can be no return to life before the deluge, yet Ursula envisions the "new germination" in which men will create a new earth in the image of their true grace of being. She sees "in the rainbow the earth's new architecture, the old, brittle corruption of houses and factories swept away, the world built up in a living fabric of Truth, fitting to the over-arching heaven."

3

Women in Love: The Last Judgment

One of Lawrence's original titles for the novel that became *Women in Love* was "The Latter Days." Writing to Catherine Carswell, he says that the book frightens him, for "it is so end of the world."[1] And indeed the passionately polemical tone of the novel—the most casual episode searching a moral, or more likely an ontological, question—reveals Lawrence as a prophet announcing the imminent "Day of Yahweh," the judgment that will surely befall a degenerate and complacent Elect. The prophet lamented his people's deviation from the known path of righteousness. Lawrence's experience was somewhat analogous: he was confronted by the double awareness of delight and wonder in the ever creative life of the world, as a primary reality, yet increasingly more strongly he found manifest demonstration of man's activity of destruction.

The letters of the early war years reveal this passion of conflict. Despairing or vehement, Lawrence rages at the war and at the war spirit he finds all around him, and exhorts his friends to join him in the formation of a renewed society based on the primary goodness that is in man. This is best epitomized, perhaps, in a letter to Lady Cynthia Asquith, written in February 1915. He describes to her the shock that the declaration of war the previous August had caused him: it was as if, Christ-like, he had been crucified and buried. Now, corpse-cold, he was beginning to feel the stirrings of resurrection. Part of this shock was caused by apprehension of the collision of beauty and destruction during those August days when, he writes, "we all went mad." He remembers the frantic patriotism of soldiers and their wives and girlfriends, the flood of factory workers beginning to be driven by the war machine. "Then," he continues:

> I went down the coast a few miles. And I think of the amazing sunsets over flat sands and the smoky sea—then of sailing in a fisherman's boat, running in the wind against a heavy sea—and a French onion boat coming in with her sails set splendidly, in the morning sunshine—and the electric suspense everywhere—and the amazing, vivid, visionary beauty of everything, heightened by the immense pain everywhere.[2]

For many of his countrymen the announcement of war aroused great patriotic fervor; the troops were sent out to fight a war of liberation, one which most felt would be over in a matter of weeks. But Lawrence from the beginning—exempted by his health from active service—refused to take any part in the war effort, never ceasing to denounce the war as unmitigated evil. There were some who while serving in the war yet agreed with Lawrence as to its spiritually disintegrative effect on those who are involved. Siegfried Sassoon, for instance, reiterating sentiments he had expressed throughout the war years, said in 1918:

> Let no one from henceforth say one word countenancing war. It is dangerous even to speak of how here and there the individual may gain some hardship of soul by it. For war is hell and those who institute it are criminals. Were there even anything to say for it it should not be said; for its spiritual disasters far outweigh any of its advantages.[3]

Embittered at the waste of lives in what he now saw as unjustifiable war, Sassoon in 1917 circulated an open letter denouncing the war that he had served in as having become not a war of defence and liberation but one of conquest and aggression.[4] But at the beginning of the war, in what seems from the hindsight of the terrible subsequent years to have been a curiously innocent elation, there were not many to agree with Lawrence's wholehearted denunciation of the war and with his refusal to have anything to with it.

As he contemplated the war, Lawrence became preoccupied with the need for social reform; for "it is no use saying a man's soul should be free, if his boots hurt him so much he can't walk."[5] He urged his friends to join him in forming a revolutionary party; he became acquainted with Bertrand Russell and persuaded Russell to give a joint course of public lectures—"he on Ethics, I on immortality." Lady Ottoline Morrell was to form the nucleus of a group of like-minded people; Garsington, her home, was to be the center from which life in the new world would be planned and entered upon. Thus was formed the idea of Rananim,[6] a cell group founded on communal resources and mutual trust. Such a group was to spearhead the new era that would dawn after the war. It would be the New Life, born phoenix-like from the holocaust. To Lady Cynthia Asquith Lawrence wrote, in January 1915: "I know we shall all come through, rise again and walk healed and whole and new in a big inheritance here on earth."[7]

In the course of the year 1915, Lawrence's sense of the physical and spiritual devastation wrought by the war took on apocalyptic forms; an era was disintegrating in violence.[8] In September 1915, he described a zeppelin raid as the apocalyptic end of the world.

> So it seems our cosmos has burst, burst at last, the stars and moon blown away, the envelope of the sky burst out, and a new cosmos appeared; with a long-ovate, gleaming central luminary, calm and drifting in a glow of light, like a new moon, with its light bursting

in flashes on the earth, to burst away the earth also. So it is the end—our world is gone, and
we are like dust in the air.

But there must be a new heaven and a new earth, a clearer, eternal moon above, and a clean
world below. So it will be.[9]

Yet the new world that he called upon his friends to initiate failed to
materialize. When Russell's lecture outline proved too liberal, secular, and
placatory for Lawrence, and his friends failed to rally to the making of
Rananim, Lawrence turned to writing a series of pamphlets, grouped as "The
Crown"; for "one must speak for life in this mess of destruction and
disintegration." The argument of "The Crown" is subtle; yet, in a somewhat
shamefaced later preface to the group of essays, Lawrence confesses his lack of
faith in the venture and its ineffectiveness, although he still stands by the
content of the essays themselves.

As these projects foundered, Lawrence began to see his key associates,
Lady Ottoline and Russell in particular, as having betrayed him:

They come to me, and they make me talk, and they enjoy it, it gives them a profoundly
gratifying sensation... as if I were a cake or a wine or a pudding.... All that is dynamic in the
world, they convert to a sensation, to the gratification of what is static.[10]

He talked of leaving for Florida, and was on the point of doing so when, in
November, *The Rainbow* was suppressed. Held up by court proceedings, he
resigned himself to remaining in England, rented an isolated cottage in
Cornwall, from which at the beginning of 1916 he wrote, in the swing of the
dialectic, "I've done bothering about the world and people."[11] The Rananim
scheme gradually revived, however: John Middleton Murry and Katherine
Mansfield were to join them in Cornwall, with Heseltine, Lady Ottoline, and
possibly even Russell, if he could cast off his intellectualism and resolve to be
simply "a creature." But the scheme had lost its fire; the disenchanted prophet
returned to the wilderness, declaring (in a letter to Lady Ottoline):

As far as I possibly can, I will stand outside this time, I will live my life, and, if possible, be
happy, though the whole world slides in horror down into the bottomless pit. There is a
greater truth than the truth of the present, there is a God beyond these gods of today. Let
them fight and fall round their idols, my fellow men: it is their affair. As for me, as far as I can,
I will save myself, for I believe that the highest virtue is to be happy, living in the greatest
truth, not submitting to the falsehood of these personal times.[12]

He no longer sought apocalyptic renewal through the remaking of his society;
but turned again to symbolic action.

In Cornwall, after some sickness during the winter, Lawrence regained his
strength, and began remaking the latter part of "The Sisters" into *Women in
Love*. The novel:

comes rapidly, and is very good. When one is shaken to the very depths, one finds reality in the unreal world. At present my real world is the world of my inner soul, which reflects on to the novel I write.[13]

In his foreword to *Women in Love* Lawrence describes his characters as being full of the bitterness of war, although the war itself is not a specific issue, the question of patriotism being only briefly discussed in the novel, at the wedding party at Shortlands. The novel's setting is apparently immediately pre- or post-war; but, as Lawrence says, implicit in the characterization and in the development of the action is his own experience of the traumatic year and a half since August 1914. In letters and in such wartime essays as "The Reality of Peace" and "The Crown" series, Lawrence tries to probe the will to war as it originates, not in political confrontation, but as a phenomenon within the individual. He writes, in November 1914, to Harriet Monroe:

The war is dreadful. It is the business of the artist to follow it home to the heart of the individual fighters—not to talk in armies and nations and numbers—but to track it home—home—their war—and it's at the bottom of almost every Englishman's heart—the war—the desire of war—the *will* to war—and at the bottom of every German's.[14]

He accuses Russell of a hypocritical sublimation of the real desire in him to destroy. For Lawrence such heartening concepts as "patriotism," "peace," and "democracy" are slogans bandied about to conceal the lust for possession that actually draws his countrymen into the war, even when, as with his Cornish acquaintances for whom he has the greatest sympathy, they are the duped victim of a false "duty to their fellow men." This, for Lawrence, will not do.

I know that if the Germans wanted my little house, I would rather give it them than fight for it: because my little house is not important enough to me. If another man must fight for his house, the more's the pity. But it is his affair. To fight for possessions, goods, is what my soul *will not* do. Therefore it will not fight for the neighbor who fights for his own goods.[15]

He can feel none of this "madness of righteousness"; no passion for his own land, in the abstract, nor for his money or his possessions. The rule of Prussia, he writes in an earlier letter, is indeed evil; but it is an external evil, and "the disintegrating process of the war has become an internal evil, so vast as to be almost unthinkable, so nearly overwhelming us, that we stand on the very brink of oblivion." Let Germany impose her rule on Europe, until such time as the good wins through again—as it will "if we can but trust it within ourselves."[16]

To the phantasmagoric abstractions of a world "which has gone mad in its sleep" Lawrence opposes another principle, the integrative process of love, which finds intrinsic connection with another being and so, wave-like, extends to all individuals. The spirit of war, on the other hand, is one in which the individual considers himself as a single unit having only extrinsic connection with others.

> If I love, then, I am in direct opposition to the principle of war. If war prevails, I do not love. If love prevails, there is no war. War is a great and necessary disintegrating autumnal process. Love is the great creative process, like spring, the making of an integral unity out of many disintegrated factors. We have had enough of the disintegrating process. [17]

Soon, he adds, it will be too late; the living tree will have withered. Writing this long statement of belief to Lady Cynthia Asquith, Lawrence confesses that he knows no men now who would be able to understand that further destruction means only "death, universal death, disintegration." He concludes that on this topic it is only to the women that he can appeal.

Support of the war is for most a dead abstraction. "I would say to my Cornishmen," Lawrence writes to Catherine Carswell, "'Don't let your house and home be a symbol of your manhood.' Because it has been the symbol for so long, it has exhausted us, become a prison. So we fight, desperate and hopeless."[19] A deeper need lies within the individual. There is, says Lawrence:

> a wish for pure, unadulterated relationship with the universe, for truth in being. My pure relationship with one woman is marriage, physical and spiritual: with another, is another form of happiness, according to our nature. And so on for ever. [19]

If "the way to immortality" is in the fulfillment of desire in pure relationship, it must also be that a pure desire for war is conceivable, Lawrence writes, adding that he would respect such desire. He further discusses this will to destruction in "The Reality of Peace" and "The Crown"; in these essays productive action is seen as arising from the dynamic opposition of the forces of integration and sundering. I shall discuss this idea more fully later in this study; now I wish only to make the point that in these essays such pure destruction is seen as being dependent on the creative movement.

> But the initial force is the force of spring, as is evident. The undoing of autumn can only follow the putting forth of spring. So that creation is primal and original, corruption is only a consequence. [20]

This belief in the primacy of the creative impulse becomes a more ambivalent, more troubled, and more powerful act of faith in the experience of the novel, just as the continuing "grain of hope" which Lawrence expresses in the letters of the time bears witness to a courage being won from months of painful and embittering experience. His struggle is manifested in the fighting tone of the poem "Craving for Spring"; only barely is hope maintained for creative renewal in the nourishing sap of spring, making new living form: "wonderment organizing itself."[21]

Individuals within the society described in *Women in Love* are possessed of those disintegrative energies that have made their culture an ugly and warlike one. The four main characters, Ursula and Gudrun, Birkin and Gerald, are people at the end of their tether. At the beginning of the novel Gudrun and Ursula sit together in their father's house, at a loss. What is there to do? Satisfaction of that indeterminate hankering which Gerald tries to articulate and which Birkin calls "fulfillment" is, the sisters feel, to be denied them. Nothing apparently comes to fruition; marriage and childbearing seem to them impossible, yet conventionally "the inevitable next step." As they break off their unhappy pondering—in fact to watch Laura Crich's wedding, an example of the "inevitable next step"—Ursula experiences a revulsion from her familiar surroundings: "She was afraid at the depth of her feeling against the home, the milieu, the whole atmosphere and condition of this obsolete life."[22]

Gudrun, freer in her way of life than her sister, has returned to Beldover as a gesture of *reculer pour mieux sauter*. Her greater bravado conceals her dismay at finding very few places it would be worthwhile to jump to. Birkin too, as we first meet him, is drifting in a kind of limbo, in confederation with Hermione, yet dissatisfied. "He moved about a great deal, his life seemed uncertain, without any definite rhythm, any organic meaning" (*WIL*, p. 45). His sickness, he explains to Ursula, results from a sickness of spirit; and she, though she maintains a facade of happiness, sees her life passing away in the dreary succession of school terms and vacations. But the writer describes also a continuing inner process: "Her spirit was active, her life a shoot that is growing steadily, but which has not yet come above ground" (*WIL*, p. 45).

It is the dark time of the year for these characters; each is ripe for death—or for rebirth, as Ursula considers it. Birkin feels himself to be at a similar crossroads. Knowing the precariousness of his health, he prefers to die rather than to live a life unsatisfactory to him. But better yet to "persist and persist and persist for ever, till one were satisfied in life" (*WIL*, p. 191).

The characters are aware of a profound hopelessness within themselves. Birkin voices this as a more extensive despair: humanity itself has come to the end of its line of life. His culture lives a lie, in that it professes love while desiring destruction. In a specifically wartime reference he says of his countrymen: "They distill themselves with nitro-glycerine, all the lot of them, out of very love. It's the lie that kills" (*WIL*, p. 143). Man is a corrupted product of a force that finds more perfect issue; he is a temporary incarnation of that impulse that creates the non-human world in beauty and completeness. "Do you think," Birkin asks,

> that creation depends on *man?* It merely doesn't. There are the trees and the grass and birds. I much prefer to think of the lark rising up in the morning upon a humanless world. Man is a mistake, he must go. There is the grass, and hares and adders, and the unseen hosts, actual angels that go about freely when a dirty humanity doesn't interrupt them—and good pure-tissued demons: very nice (*WIL*, p. 120).

Birkin's is a powerful evocation of what Gerard Manley Hopkins called "the dearest freshness deep down things," which man has managed to blear, smear with toil. Yet the image of renewal as being that of a pristine world purged of men is countered by Ursula and countered in the action of the novel.

A similar argument with Gerald in the train going to London represents Birkin's view of the lie that man lives today. "We have an ideal of a perfect world," Birkin exclaims, "clean and straight and sufficient. So we cover the earth with foulness; life is a blotch of labor, like insects scurrying in filth, so that your collier can have a pianoforte in his parlor, . . ." (*WIL*, p. 47). We make our world as we desire it.

Elsewhere, in like manner, Birkin denounces his culture's spiritual bankruptcy; but these two examples sufficiently make the point that both within the individual life rhythm and within the structures of society the characters find themselves at the end of an era. The end-of-the-world character of the novel goes deeper, however, exploring not only the characters' articulation of apocalypse but also their deeper understanding of psychic destruction and possible renewal.

The apocalyptic action of the novel, the action of those living—as they (and the author) understand it—in the Last Days, must involve a judgment, a judgment based on the life choices each character makes in the course of the novel. Therefore the four chief characters are confronted with similar crucial decisions, as they find themselves at the same crossroads. These dilemmas turn primarily on matters of human relationship, especially the choice of a marriage partner. Each meets the question in his characteristic fashion, handles it according to his present understanding of reality. In the eschatological dimension of Lawrence's vision, this is literally a matter of life and death, and yet it is also a choice which remains always open to be remade.

Birkin and Gerald have also to consider the question of a commitment to each other, a matter of great importance particularly to Birkin. At various points the opportunity of real intimacy opens to Gerald; each time he verges on acceptance of Birkin's love, each time he retreats to his inviolate isolation. The writer presents each such moment as a Last Judgment; the final one culminates in physical death and the terrible isolation in death that Birkin sees manifest in the body of his friend.

Both kinds of relationship, man to woman and man to man, depend on the nature of the reality each character finds to be central to his living. When Birkin asks Gerald about this, Gerald replies that he is unable to find any center intrinsic to himself. Life is "artificially held *together* by the social mechanism." Birkin for his part maintains that he needs as a base "one pure single activity"— and this he believes he will find in love, in the committedness to a woman that he calls "ultimate marriage" (*WIL*, p. 51). Upon the ground of action outlined here by the two men the life and death judgment depends.

Since the four main characters confront parallel choices, since the two women are sisters and the two men friends, they have many of the same associates and do many things together. The plot therefore has a conciseness that binds together the many different aspects of the culture that it discusses: the industrial mining town of Beldover and the world of its master, Shortlands; the aristocratic way of life as found at Breadalby; the bourgeois tedium of the sisters' own home (altered somewhat from the vivid Brangwen household of *The Rainbow*); avant-garde Bohemia; and the snowed-in Tyrolean hostel that repeats England's decadence, in a Continental mode, in the person of Loerke.[23]

Lawrence's plot also takes on a characteristically circling movement; or—more accurately—since there is also the onward direction of narrative, the movement of a helix; in fact, since it is the account of two pairs of characters, a double helix. The analogy is not complete: one important movement of narrative is that of the ebb and flow of the relationship between Birkin and Gerald, a movement breaking the double spiral, or forming a spiral of different constituents, though with the same circling and ongoing motion.

The circle often revolves around a place or situation which, in the eschatological drama of the novel, each person understands after his own fashion. Whenever a Last Judgment begins, Blake said, "its Vision is seen by the Imaginative Eye of Every one according to the situation he holds."[24]

Breadalby, for example, creates such a focus. We see the place first through the eyes of the sisters, patronized by Hermione; their feelings toward the place are understandably mingled. They are enchanted by the graciousness, peace, and beauty of the house and gardens. Yet, connected as it is with Hermione's officious bounty, they resent its completeness, its finished excellence, that very peace and mellow beauty, that sense of a privileged place that they so admire. They find Hermione's friends wearisome; conversation is "a canal, not a stream." Analytical and satiric, the talk, of which there is much, turns mainly on political and sociological matters; Ursula imagines a witch's pot of poisonous brew stoked and stirred by Hermione, Birkin, and the saurian Joshua (Lawrence's revenge on Russell). Hermione, in withered domination, marshalls her guests through activities appropriate to her advanced intellectual-Bohemian house party. The event is *voulu;* yet the atmosphere has undeniable beauty, and such aristocratic assurance beguiles the visitors.

Birkin, too, has mixed feelings. He is a center of that corrosive argument that the sisters find so painful; yet he derides such talk. He admires the country house and its leisured and graceful way of life, and yet repudiates the outworn aristocratic tradition. Birkin's double sense of the beauty and the confinement of Breadalby reflects Lawrence's anguished feelings at this time towards Garsington, Lady Ottoline's home, a milieu much like Hermione's and the one on which Breadalby—though not its physical location—was based. As I mentioned in the preceding chapter, Lawrence sees Lady Ottoline's home as representative of a dying era, the accomplished past which must, like overripe fruit, fall from the tree at last. For Birkin, life at Breadalby follows a worn-out tradition; it is an overplayed game, not authentic play. For Lawrence, more indirectly, Garsington was the perfected image of the farming countryside of his youth, from which, in the course of 1915, he knew he must exile himself; it is also the image of a dying culture that is beautiful and desirable, and in which war is a terrible but final aberration.

In Birkin Lawrence portrays a man who finds less pain in the repudiation of a traditional past than did his author. This is perhaps because in the novel Lawrence chose to focus on the living representative of those who made the proportioned grace of Breadalby. In Hermione he represents a woman whose values, actions, and feelings are those of will and habit: she bullies herself, as she subtly bullies others.

Gerald's action at Breadalby is much like Hermione's; he slides into the values of the past without questioning the reality of his ideas, as he would according to a more living apprehension. Thus he is attracted to Gudrun, yet is only partly persuaded by Birkin that the two girls, despite their being of a lower social class, are worth his notice. The cohesive social mechanism of which he had spoken to Birkin on the London train operates here to censor any interest he has in Gudrun. In the same way he is, later, to make much to-do about a formal payment to Minette that he neglected after sleeping with her for several nights. These are the conventions that hold the self together. It is the same for Hermione, whose social position is the only guarantee of whatever tenuous sense of herself she has.

> No one could put her down, no one could make mock of her, because she stood among the first, and those that were against her were below her, either in rank, or in wealth, or in high association of thought and progress and understanding. So, she was invulnerable. All her life she had sought to make herself invulnerable, unassailable, beyond reach of the world's judgment.
> And yet her soul was tortured, exposed.... (*WIL,* p. 10).

The chapter "Water Party" in similar fashion constellates image and action around a central theme: the annual water party of Thomas Crich. The various events ebb and flow in parallel motion around the image, a celebration and a tragedy; as the lake is alternately peaceful, a place to swim and row, and menacing, a deathly underworld. So, after a lyrical afternoon, the two girls move into events of contrary motion. The innocent singing of Ursula develops into Gudrun's strange ritual dance before the cattle whom she goads to attack and whose savage instincts metamorphose into the figure of Gerald, appearing suddenly to receive Gudrun's challenge. At the same time the little marsh beside which the sisters picnic in childlike innocence early in the evening later becomes Birkin's river of darkness "putting forth lilies and snakes, and the ignis fatuus, and rolling all the time onward" (*WIL,* pp. 163-64). Ursula's tentative song is transposed by Birkin into the rhythm of a grotesque dance, abandoned, satiric, and licentious.

As night falls, they light marvelously colored paper lanterns that reveal strange and beautiful forms, yet scarcely illuminate the night, so that as they row, the dark lake and their gentle motion creates a magic stasis—until this is shattered by the fall of Diana. The water then becomes a vast underworld deadly and illimitable to the horror-struck watchers—to Gerald, insidiously attractive as an empty universe in which he finds himself alone and free. Gudrun recognizes that Gerald is in his element: "It was as if he belonged naturally to dread and catastrophe, as if he were himself again" (*WIL*, p. 171). There is a sense in which Gerald exults in the realm of death that he finds as he dives for the drowning pair, the dark expanse that has now become the "river of dissolution." Birkin himself is fascinated by the great race of water as it pours over the sluice emptying the lake; as he watches he becomes one with the dissolutive process that he has just tried to draw Gerald from. His absorption frightens Ursula, who fights the lure of

> a heavy, booming noise of a great body of water falling solidly all the time. It occupied the whole of the night, this great steady booming of water, everything was drowned within it, drowned and lost. Ursula seemed to have to struggle for her life (*WIL*, p. 177).

Yet from this experience of death comes rebirth, the affirmation of their love. Their physical passion revokes that death that each had seen in himself as he witnessed the accident; it is the rebirth which Birkin had described as an escape from the "life that belongs to death," the drift in which he sees himself caught. And so in its delicate tenderness their subsequent lovemaking forms an image for the reader of an alternative to the dark lake of death and the booming water. It is the rainbow after the deluge, the covenant of faith that denies the splendor of isolation found by Gerald in the deep water and apprehended by Birkin at the sluice, as earlier, at Breadalby, while rolling in the pristine isolation of wet vegetation.

Thus around the tragic celebration there move in like movement images of innocence and corruption, of celebration and death, of creation and separation, isolation and relationship.

"Classroom" establishes that atmosphere of growth and nurturance with which Ursula is connected. The sense of early spring is felt through the description of the pale golden light, and the unhurried purposeful activity of the classroom contrasts with the harshness created by Birkin's entrance. The classroom forms an appropriate setting for the emotional argument that develops between Birkin and Hermione, in the course of which Birkin demolishes Hermione's sentimental understanding of knowledge as a hindrance to sensitive awareness. For Birkin there is the knowledge of phenomena outside ourselves which we have no right to draw into the circle of our emotional subjectivity—as, for instance, the botanical facts that Ursula has just been explaining to her students. This is one aspect of that ability to lose one's self-conscious egocentricity that Birkin goes on to explain to Ursula in the idea of "lapsing out": "You've got to learn not-to-be, before you can come into being" (*WIL*, p. 37). In this chapter an idea important to the novel is outlined: the question of the centrality of the ego; and the battle lines are drawn up— Birkin in conflict with Hermione and, in part, with Ursula. But, appropriately for its setting, the dialogue is a dramatized lecture. It will be substantiated or qualified in the later images of the novel. But we notice that the discussion has a pedagogical tone appropriate to this stage in the plot's development; and this derives from the central image: a botany lesson towards the close of an afternoon in early spring.

One could multiply examples of the circling narrative movement; "The Industrial Magnate" and "Continental," for instance, function in such a way, polarizing the participants according to their understanding of what is real or superficial. Lawrence has an interesting comment to make on his method in his last book, *Apocalypse*. The comment does not directly refer to his own writing, but well illustrates his method. He describes the pagan writer as thinking in images: he "starts with an image, sets the image in motion, allows it to achieve a certain course or circuit of its own, and then takes up another image." Such a narrative requires a different understanding of time:

> To appreciate the pagan manner of thought we have to drop our own manner of on-and-on-and-on, from a start to a finish, and allow the mind to move in cycles, or to flit here and there over a cluster of images. Our ideas of time as a continuity in an eternal straight line has crippled our consciousness cruelly. The pagan conception of time as moving in cycles is much freer, it allows movement upwards and downwards, and allows for a complete change of the state of mind, at any moment.[25]

Earlier in *Apocalypse,* writing of the pagan oracles, Lawrence says: "They were supposed to deliver a set of images or symbols of the real dynamic value, which should set the emotional consciousness of the enquirer, as he pondered them, revolving more and more rapidly, till out of a state of intense emotional absorption the resolve at last formed; or, as we say, the decision was arrived at."[26]

In *Women in Love* Lawrence draws on the potency of the image as center of the meditative activity; and, since his medium is narrative, that circling becomes the motion of a cylindrical spiral. The "completed thought," as the plumbing of a depth of emotional awareness in which the resolve is formed, is the moment of realization in which the participant makes his decision without being aware that he has done so. Thus, the lovemaking of Birkin and Ursula in the scenes of "Water-Party" which I have just discussed results from their discussion of the rivers of life and disolution, from the tragedy they have witnessed, from the beauty of the magical evening before the drowning and the earlier insouciant afternoon, from the great deluge of the lake emptying; as well as—but not only because of—their growing feeling of love towards each other. These things have come together, not in rational consciousness but as the moment of "a completed state of feeling awareness."

It is important to add that this is no static completeness. "All our mental consciousness is a movement onwards, a movement in stages, like our sentences, and every full-stop is our arrival somewhere."[27] As Lawrence describes the primitive way of thinking, and as he himself sees the process, a decision, an insight, is found to be lost again and found, in a continuous process. Thus, after the peace of their meeting, Ursula sinks into a profound despair, a point of light only remaining in her spirit; Birkin comes to her home to find her hard in rejection. The novel ends in doubt, but that doubt does not invalidate the achievement of Birkin and Ursula; it is the ebb in an underlying process. "Many arrivals make us live" (wrote Theodore Roethke); *Women in Love,* like *The Rainbow,* is a series of birthings and dyings—for "love is strictly a traveling."

Not only in love but in any real connection with the world, there is the process, the many arrivals, the traveling.

> Life, the ever-present, knows no finality, no finished crystallization. The perfect rose is only a running flame, emerging and flowing off, and never in any sense at rest, static, finished. Herein lies its transcendent loveliness. The whole tide of all life and all time suddenly heaves, and appears before us as an apparition, a revelation. We look at the very white quick of nascent creation. A water-lily heaves herself from the flood, looks around, gleams, and is gone. We have seen the incarnation, the quick of the ever-swirling flood.[28]

Lawrence sees his characters as living in the Last Days; they are to decide for life or death. Therefore there is an interesting question as to the degree and kind of freedom allotted to them. To what degree is a person seen in this novel as free to create the world in the image of his desire—to "save himself," in other words—or as responsible for his own psychic or physical death? How far is he bound by the circumstances of his past life or his social environment?

Birkin expresses a belief in radical freedom; he maintains that "people only do what they want to do—and what they are capable of doing" (*WIL,* p. 48). That capability is essentially an understanding of the world as founded—as he puts it elsewhere—on "pure relationships" purged of the need to base one's living on possession of people or things. England is in its present ugly state because this is what the individuals composing the body politic want. As Birkin declares to Gerald: "When we really want to go for something better we shall smash the old" (*WIL,* p. 47). Later in the conversation he says that one can and must create the world according to one's desire. This is why he sees his discovery of Ursula as the finding of a new world.

In *Women in Love* we see the beginning of something that is even more clearly manifest in the later fiction, the elitist sense of the elect as the saved remnant. For instance, the couple to whom Birkin and Ursula give a chair, a man and woman representative of the ordinary world, are seen as creatures of another realm, described in animal imagery: he, for instance, is throughout the meeting seen as a rat. The ordinary people, though living in psychic death, will inherit a moribund earth; Ursula and Birkin and their like must live in the chinks that are left them. Lawrence's espousal of the idea of a predetermined hopelessness for those who will "inherit the earth"—the "mass" of men—sits uneasily with the broad range of freedom within which the other characters make their decisions.

Birkin's understanding of radical freedom is countered by Ursula, who has greater comprehension of the mingling of what Yeats called Chance and Choice. For example, in the mountains, as a cowshed door opens, she is reminded suddenly of her childhood, of Marsh Farm; and a bitter wave of resentment rolls over her as she reflects on the toilsome journey that her life has been to bring her to this place.

> She wanted to have no past. She wanted to have come down from the slopes of heaven to this place, with Birkin, not to have toiled out of the murk of her childhood and her upbringing, slowly, all soiled (*WIL,* p. 399).

But she knows that history can only be incorporated in the "new birth," not repudiated. Thus the visionary hope for rebirth is tempered by a gritty sense of the reality of one's history, just as the moments of accord or of insight come momentarily, and attend upon the ebb of doubt or denial. Lawrence does not neglect the constraints of history; acknowledgment of such limitation, as offered by Ursula, provides the necessary qualification of Birkin's position and thus frees the reader to contemplate that stance.

Gerald, on the other hand, is bound within a self-confinement that he sees as having been long ago determined for himself and the entire Crich family. As a child he had accidentally killed his brother, and he believes himself to bear the mark of Cain; his image of himself as ineluctably drawn towards destruction proves to be self-fulfilling. For Gerald, Diana's drowning is a necessary step in the Criches' destiny, and as such is almost satisfying to him. "Once anything goes wrong," he says, "it can never be put right again—not with us" (*WIL,* p. 176). So he will act not out of inner need but from convention or habit. The possibility of relationship that radically changes a person he sees as an improbable fancy.

The plot of the novel is founded on Birkin's assertion of radical freedom; and Lawrence himself, outside the novel, comes close to such belief. For instance, in a letter to Lady Cynthia Asquith he insists that the individual is not bound to existing conditions.

> Every living soul believes that the conditions will be modified to its own growth or expression. Every living soul believes that all things real are within the scope of a Great Will which is working itself out in all things, but also and most vitally in the soul itself.[29]

His criticism of Tolstoy and of Hardy, whom he discussed in detail in this connection, was that these writers finally had little faith in the power of the individual to change his world, in other words to live his life as he really desired it, "to persist and persist and persist for ever," as Birkin says, "till one [is] satisfied in life" (*WIL*, p. 191).

In *Women in Love*, as in his other writings, Lawrence finds inadequate a deterministic position such as that of Gerald, who fights Birkin's imagination of freedom. To a greater degree than in most other writers, Lawrence's characters are responsible for the quality of choice between true and false ways of life, even—in these days—between life and death. In the foreword to *Women in Love* he writes:

> The creative, spontaneous soul sends forth its promptings of desire and aspiration in us. These promptings are our true fate, which is our business to fulfil. A fate dictated from outside, from theory or from circumstance, is a false fate.

It is not clear whether Lawrence is here writing of his characters or of his own understanding of the inner promptings that grew to be *Women in Love;* but it would in any case be true for him of both characters' destiny and the act of writing.

A different kind of freedom obtains in a writer like Henry James. Perhaps James's characters are no less free than those of Lawrence, but their freedom is of another sort. It is the option to perceive ever more clearly, although one may be powerless to change the course of events. The achievement is to see with more sympathy the inner directives of another, loosing the bonds of the self-circumscribed limitations of vision. Thus in *The Wings of the Dove,* Densher's discovery, and his heroism, lie in his gradual understanding of Milly's perfectly lucid nature, to which he then owes allegiance, though this allegiance takes the form largely of compassionate onlooking. So Strether, at the end of *The Ambassadors,* finds that nothing is changed; yet all who come in contact with him recognize, and are themselves changed by, that generous imagination that has been developing in him during the course of the action.

The coincidence of Choice and Chance of which Lawrence writes in the previously quoted letter to Lady Asquith becomes, in *Women in Love,* the ground of judgment. One is free to choose life or death—a life of continuing renewal in relationships based on faith or a drift in cynicism towards negation and finally despair or physical death. Lawrence himself had much of the fighting spirit of persistence he attributes to Birkin; these difficulties and limitations in the life experience are taken account of in the narrative by the very nature of its mode as a visionary novel: this is not the representation of actuality, but the fictive model of a way of being that would be impossible to achieve in any literal way. The radical freedom allowed the characters, their choices, the extremity of the judgment—these are not a mimesis of actual events but the formalization of action into the parabolic symbol. Thus a plot which is, after all, simply the same kind of story as *Middlemarch* or *Vanity Fair*—a double love story—becomes in Lawrence's hands an eschatological drama. The perfect freedom envisaged by Birkin with Ursula, in "star equilibrium," is an imaginative possibility, a lure, none the less true and real for being impossible of fulfillment in the world outside the parabolic. It is only by bringing to symbolic articulation the tendency glimpsed in the actual world that this reality can be discerned.

When Catherine Carswell asked Lawrence why he wrote of people "so sophisticated and 'artistic' and spoiled that it could hardly matter what they did and saw," he replied that only in such people could be grasped a more general tendency. "There, at the uttermost tips of the flower of an epoch's achievement, one could already see the beginning of the flower of putrefaction which must take place before the seed of the new was ready to fall clear."[30] Extrapolating a reality from a tendency, Lawrence creates, for example, the grotesque, powerful truth of Hermione from Lady Ottoline Morrell, the friend to whom he was at the same time writing with great amicability. Lawrence habitually treated his friends in this way; almost none of them escaped unburned, and in some cases they understood his action as betrayal.

"Whenever any Individual Rejects Error and Embraces Truth," wrote William Blake, "a Last Judgment passes upon that Individual."[31] The immanent judgement, articulated in the Christian model of the Last Judgment, divides the world into sinners and saved. In Lawrence, however, this judgement is seen as deriving less from a moral than from an ontological choice. For instance, in the conversation in the London train already referred to, Gerald, replying to Birkin's question "Wherein does life centre for you?" can only invoke the "social mechanism." Birkin seems to agree: "I know, it just doesn't centre. The old ideals are dead as nails—nothing there." Then, pondering further, he goes on: "It seems to me there remains only this perfect union with a woman—sort of ultimate marriage—and there isn't anything else" (*WIL*, p. 51). This exchange brings into focus a basic question in the novel, and it reveals the essential divergence of the two men. The working out of this question of centering in the choice of marriage partner and the possibility of relationship that will be of final importance—these are matters that depend on the characters' basic address on the world, how each sees his place in it.

In his work Gerald devotes himself to making things function with the greatest efficiency; out of the mines he creates a model of his understanding of the world as matter to be subjugated:

> There were two opposites, his will and the resistant Matter of the earth. And between these he could establish the very expression of his will, the incarnation of his power, a great and perfect machine, a system, an activity of pure order, pure mechanical repetition, repetition ad infinitum hence eternal and infinite (*WIL*, p. 220).

Acting from the same principle, he forces his recalcitrant Arab mare to stand at the railway crossing. Swimming, he finds himself in a lonely, powerful element that is his to control: "He loved his own vigorous, thrusting motion, and the violent impulse of the very cold water against his limbs, buoying him up" (*WIL,* p. 40). He finds extreme mechanical mastery in skiing and toboganning, until it seems that in motion he has become perfectly instrumental.

His association with Gudrun is also one of instrumentality. Thus, beset by the tensions after his father's death, he comes to her "for vindication."

> She let him hold her in his arms, clasp her close against him. He found in her an infinite relief. Into her he poured all his pent-up darkness and corrosive death, and he was whole again. It was wonderful, marvelous, it was a miracle. This was the ever-recurrent miracle of his life, at the knowledge of which he was lost in an ecstasy of relief and wonder. And she, subject, received him as a vessel filled with his bitter potion of death (*WIL,* p. 337).

Their interchange continues to be that of user and used, always "this eternal see-saw, one destroyed that the other might exist, one ratified because the other was nulled" (*WIL,* p. 436).

In the "godlike" activity of his life, which is the subduing of his world of function, Gerald finds that within the interstices of his will lurk monsters of fear, which rise up as he contemplates the purpose of his energetic activity and, later, his father's dying.

> His mind was very active. But it was like a bubble floating in the darkness. At any moment it might burst and leave him in chaos. He would not die. He knew that. He would go on living, but the meaning would have collapsed out of him, his divine reason would be gone. In a strangely indifferent, sterile way, he was frightened. But he could not react even to the fear. It was as if his centers of feeling were drying up. He remained calm, calculative and healthy, and quite freely deliberate, even whilst he felt, with faint, small but final sterile horror, that his mystic reason was breaking, giving way now, at this crisis (*WIL,* p. 225).

"I do think," says Birkin, in contrast, "that the world is only held together by the mystic conjunction, the ultimate unison between people—a bond. And the immediate bond is between man and woman" (*WIL,* p. 143). Birkin persists in fighting for this world of relationship in faith, a faith which manifests itself consistently—as does Gerald's contrary understanding of reality—in acts and decisions. Such is his search for a real commitment to Ursula, his need for intimacy with Gerald, and his responsiveness to the natural world.

The difference between the realities of the two men is indirectly presented earlier in Lawrence's work, as if prefiguring Birkin and Gerald. Though I discussed the scene in detail in an earlier section, I should like to recapitulate my argument. When Ursula, at the end of *The Rainbow,* walks in the rain through the woods and encounters the angry horse herd, we have another manifestation of those attributes of fixedness, knottedness, and rigidity that in the later novel are Gerald's reality, and which Ursula in *The Rainbow* must circumvent, as against the fluidity, lightness, and fresh response of Birkin's world, that is the lustration of wind and rain in the episode in *The Rainbow*.

A comment by Lawrence apropos of the paintings of an acquaintance, Duncan Grant, reveals what at first sight seems to be a somewhat grandiose conception of his own work as a writer.

> He is after stating the Absolute—like Fra Angelico in the "Last Judgment"—a whole conception of the existence of man—creation, good, evil, life, death, resurrection, the separating of the stream of good and evil, and its return to the eternal source. It is an Absolute we are all after, a statement of the whole scheme—the issue, the progress through time—and the return—making unchangeable eternity.[32]

Yet when the novel is seen as figuring an eschatological drama, the comment becomes clearer. Any statement of "the whole scheme" involves consideration of good and evil, and a judgment on this: "the separating of the stream of good and evil, and its return to the origin, the source." It is not clear whether Lawrence is thinking of a single stream of good and evil, or two streams— probably the latter, since he writes in the context of a reference to Fra Angelico's *Last Judgment*.

Lawrence evidently much admired this painting; he discusses it in some detail in *The Rainbow*.[33] In the fresco the Last Judgment is represented as a division of sinners and saved, moving from the coffin at the center of the painting. The depiction of the sinners tumbling hellwards and the fiery scene of Hell itself is rather soft, with none of the nightmare quality of Grünewald or Bosch. Nearer to Fra Angelico's imagination is the Entry of the Blessed, who, joining hands, wind in colorful procession through the flowering meadows of Paradise, caught up in what Anna Brangwen describes as "the real real angelic melody." This side of the painting, the stream of the Blessed, is a wonderful achievement. Though poised on the edge of the *faux-naif,* it is inescapably innocent.

Such radiance of innocence, connected as it is with his sense of Ursula, is in Birkin's mind as he contemplates their life together. He has been reflecting on the lure of a purely unmindful sensuality, whether it be the gratification of the burning caress of fire, as he saw it represented in Halliday's statue of an African woman in labor, or, as it would be expressed in the North, the sensuality of snow death. In other words: merging or isolation—the loss of the self by absorption into the being of another or the freezing of the self within the impervious and increasingly isolate ego: Birkin's own temptation. Then his mind resolves itself suddenly:

> There was another way, the way of freedom. There was the paradisal entry into pure, single being, the individual soul taking precedence over love and desire for union, stronger than any

pangs of emotion, a lovely state of free proud singleness, which accepted the obligation of the permanent connection with others, and with the other, submits to the yoke and leash of love, but never forfeits its own proud individual singleness, even while it loves and yields (*WIL*, p. 247).

Such is the fight for singleness of self which is yet in permanent, and changing, relationship with the other. This to his mind is the ground of his connection with Ursula, and, Lawrence implies, though Birkin resists such generalization, the ground of his culture's salvation.

Birkin meditates upon these two directions of relationship: the Paradisal Entry and that sensual fulfillment in which "the goodness, the holiness, and desire for creation and productive happiness... have lapsed" (*WIL*, p. 245). They seem to him to be two alternative paths. Elsewhere, talking to Ursula, he sees the same dualistic motion as two rivers. Rivers or paths, it is in their complex mingling and separation that Lawrence argues the dialectic of his novel.

For Fra Angelico the plot of his painting was clear enough: the two directions of sinners and saved obviously in opposition, the manner of motion distinguished as chaotically tumbling or circling in ordered procession. The traditional beliefs represented in Fra Angelico's painting, had for Lawrence, been lost; the two paths or streams to Heaven or Hell flow often together. Nonetheless, it is a life-and-death matter still, as it was for Fra Angelico, to know, in so far as one is able, the tendency, the constitution of the river of life and the river of dissolution.

Let every man search in his own soul to find there the quick suggestion, whether his soul be quick for life or quick for death. Then let him act as he finds it. For the greatest of all misery is a lie; and if a man belongs to the line of obstinate death, he has at least the satisfaction of pursuing this line simply. But we will not call this peace. There is all the world of difference between the sharp, drug-delicious satisfaction or resignation and self-gratifying humility and the true freedom of peace. Peace is when I accept life; when I accept death I have the hopeless equivalent of peace, which is quiescence and resignation.[34]

The alternative paths contemplated by Birkin in the reflections I have outlined found earlier expression in a discussion with Ursula, in the chapter called "Water Party." They are standing beside a little stream flowing through a marsh. The brackish smell is a source of alarm to Birkin, reminding him of a reality most choose to ignore: "It seethes and seethes, a river of darkness, putting forth lilies and snakes, and the ignis fatuus, and rolling all the time onward." We prefer to consider what is yet today an inferior reality to us: "the silver river of life, rolling on and quickening all the world to a brightness, on and on to heaven, flowing into a bright eternal sea, a heaven of angels thronging" (*WIL*, p. 164). Again the image recalls Fra Angelico's "Entry of the Blessed."

Ursula resists his characterizing of the two of them as *fleurs du mal,*
saying:

> "I think I am a rose of happiness."
> "Ready-made?" he asked ironically.
> "No—real," she said, hurt.
> "If we are the end, we are not the beginning," he said.
> "Yes we are," she said, "The beginning comes out of the end."
> "After it, not out of it. After us, not out of us."
> "You are a devil, you know, really," she said. "You want to destroy our hope. You *want* us
> to be deathly."
> "No," he said, "I only want us to *know* what we are."
> "Ha!" she cried in anger. "You only want us to know death."
> "You're quite right," said the soft voice of Gerald, out of the dusk behind (*WIL,* p. 165).

The dialogue of Birkin and Ursula turns on apocalyptic renewal. In the
parabolic structure of the book as a series of eschatological choices made by the
characters, choices which save them or damn them, Birkin here denies the very
possibility of salvation, denies that their love for each other may have
redemptive power. He denies too what he elsewhere affirms, that it is within the
power of the individual to create his own world in the image of his desire.
Ursula resists his argument, and her opposition expresses the dialectic that runs
through the book: Is the love each discovers for the other the founding of a
creative life of self-integrity or another unproductive gesture of despair?

Certainly Birkin himself is deeply implicated in the death drive of his
culture. His association with Hermione and with her circle at Breadalby is one
that he would denounce; a matter of the will clinging to worn-out forms. He
sticks to the "arty" London set that he reviles as decadent, being at ease in their
company, as we see from the scenes in Halliday's apartment. He fights
commitment to Ursula in a way that he elsewhere rejects—through argument
and self-assertion. Whereas he insists that "you've got to... lapse into
unknowingness, and give up your volition" (*WIL,* p. 37), this, and more in
similar vein, is delivered in a series of lectures; and as he harangues Ursula, he
forgets the real blossoming of sympathy between them. There is, as Ursula
points out, a gap between his expressed beliefs and his consistency in living
them. Deriding Hermione's way of life as *voulu,* he is himself charged with a
self-will that is opposed in deliberate and often forced resistance to his
associates. A man advocating silence and distrust of the word, he never ceases
to lecture and argue with his friends.

At a deeper level, he possesses that rage for destruction which Lawrence
reveals in letters at this time—the will to smash and destroy, as in the argument
with Ursula in which he expresses satisfaction in contemplating the imminent
apocalypse. In another aspect, this is the longing for isolation, the severing of
all human relationships, which is another version of Gerald's snow death: the
isolation of the heart.

Nor is it simply Birkin who, though unquestionably representing a positive force, is yet deeply immersed in the river of dissolution. Ursula, too, hard in her egotistic resistance, is moved almost to death by a despair at the ennui of her life. These two share the culture's self-destructive energies; yet Lawrence represents their fighting love as a positive movement. If they are not yet roses—in Birkin's words—"warm and flamy," there remains the possibility of such blossoming. Gudrun and Gerald, on the other hand, are, as Birkin says, born "in the process of destructive creation."

Gudrun is possessed of a perfect self-consciousness in which every action, every event, becomes ironical; every confrontation is shaped by her imagination into a finished thing apart from herself, analyzed into an image. Thus she views the Criches at the wedding of Laura, thus she considers her acquaintances, thus she holds Gerald at a distance, maintains a final reserve towards her sister, considers the suitability of her conduct after the death of Gerald's sister, and again at Gerald's own death. It is for her a desolating sense: "Ursula seemed so peaceful and sufficient unto herself, sitting there unconsciously crooning her song, strong and unquestioned at the center of her own universe" (*WIL*, p. 157). During the final traumatic days and nights in an Austrian hostel, she suffers the consummation of her ironical view of reality, in which all hope and desire crumble to ash. In an agony of self-consciousness she sees herself as eternally fixed within a meaningless chronology.

> She must always see and know and never escape. She could never escape. There she was, placed before the clock-face of life. And if she turned round as in a railway station to look at the book-stall, still she could see, with her very spine, she could see the clock, always the great white clock-face. In vain she fluttered the leaves of books, or made statuettes in clay. She knew she was not *really* reading. She was not *really* working. She was watching the fingers twitch across the eternal, mechanical, monotonous clock-face of time (*WIL*, pp. 456-57).

And yet Lawrence presents Gudrun's understanding with profound sympathy, as part of his own reality. (His "Pansies," for example, often express Gudrun's sense of the world.) In the above passage and in many others, such as that in which Gudrun imagines individuals as cogwheels eternally turning one with the other in futile activity as part of a great meaningless machine, Lawrence's writing has great power. Further, he portrays Gudrun as having much intrinsic beauty, as evinced, for example, by Ursula's comment: "There was a certain playfulness about her too, such a piquancy or ironic suggestion, such an untouched reserve" (*WIL*, p. 4). Her stylish manner of dress is part of the bravura, the vitality with which Lawrence invests Gudrun.

In her ironic understanding of reality, Gudrun resembles Gerald: both see themselves, finally, as only extrinsically connected to others. We remember that, writing to Lady Cynthia in 1915, Lawrence had discussed this sense of being a single entity having "no intrinsic reference to the rest" as basic to the spirit of war. On the other hand, "Love is the great creative process like Spring, the making of an integral unity out of many disintegrated factors."[35] Thus Gudrun and Gerald embody the characteristics that create war between individuals—between the two of them, between Gerald and his horse, and his workers—and therefore within a society. An individual in a relationship of trust creates an integral unity opposed to war. Gudrun and Gerald embody the fatal isolation of the self that is common in Lawrence's apprehension of his countrymen, and about which he says:

> If it goes on any further, we shall so thoroughly have destroyed the unifying force from among us, we shall have become each one of us so completely a separate entity, that the whole will be an amorphous heap, like sand, sterile, hopeless, useless, like a dead tree.[36]

As a boy Lawrence had noticed that among the mining community the men, intuitive in their dark underground life, had often a curiously meditative streak, were often content to contemplate a flower and move on, whereas their women must pick the flower, gather it to themselves. Gerald's lack of central self is the obverse of a will to power, evinced in his handling of the mines and in his association with Gudrun. Similarly Hermione, who habitually patronizes her friends, desires always to possess, to draw into herself, people, things, ideas. Birkin angrily denounces her acquisitive consciousness:

> Your passion is a lie. It isn't passion at all, it is your *will*. It's your bullying will. You want to clutch things and have them in your power. You want to have things in your power. And why? Because you haven't got any real body, any dark sensual body of life. You have no sensuality. You have only your will and your conceit of consciousness, and your lust for power, to *know* (*WIL*, p. 35).

Another manifestation of the craving for power is the lust for material possessions that Birkin censures in his argument with Gerald in the London train: "Life is a blotch of labor, like insects scurrying in filth, so that your collier can have a pianoforte in his parlour" (*WIL*, p. 47). So in letters of the period again and again Lawrence reviles this "dragon that has devoured us all: . . . this insatiable struggle and desire to possess, to possess always and in spite of everything, this need to be an owner, lest one be owned."[37] Gerald and Hermione incarnate that lust for ownership that destroys the selfhood of the individual and withers culture.

Thomas Crich, however, is worse; for he embodies the hypocrisy that Lawrence found everywhere in the talk of patriotism and peace, as I described it earlier in this chapter. Crich's natural hostility has been converted into a philanthropy maintained by a monstrous firmness of will. His wife is poisoned by the venomous fruit of his love, as in Blake's "A Poison Tree." So Bertrand Russell, too, from Lawrence's viewpoint, spoke for war under the guise of democracy and peace, being full of hatred.

The most extreme degeneration in human relationship is represented by Loerke, the German painter in whom Gudrun finds intelligence beyond Gerald's. Loerke is Gerald without the illusions—or humanity—that remains as a possible area of growth (or weakness) in Gerald's world. For Loerke is perfectly skeptical. He embraces with alluring intelligence the model of a purely mechanical life of subjection to the machine; thus his colossal granite sculpture portrays workers at a fair lost to one another in a frenzy of mechanical motion. Curiously enough, in his perfect skepticism, he shows an insouciance that is not unlike Birkin's: a hellish parody of the detachment that Birkin seeks. Loerke and Gudrun meet in ironic intelligence, mocking through parody those values that Ursula and Birkin reach for: "It was a sentimental delight [for them] to reconstruct the world of Goethe at Weimar, or of Schiller and poverty and faithful love. . . ." (*WIL*, p. 444). The vision of disaster contemplated by Birkin becomes a playful fantasy to Loerke: the catastrophic end of the world in ice.

Loerke has, however, a grotesque attraction for Lawrence, as prophetic witness of an extreme of decadence, to which, however, he will not submit. His art and his theory of art meet the resistance of Ursula and Birkin; and he is described through images of small repulsive creatures, as a rat in a sewer. There is energy in Loerke, but none of that awe with which Lawrence regarded the work of Mark Gertler, a prototype of Loerke. "I *do* think," he wrote in a letter to Gertler,

> that in this combination of blaze, and violent mechanized rotation and complete involution, and ghastly, utterly mindless human intensity of sensational extremity, you have made a real and ultimate revelation. . . . I realise how superficial your human relationships must be, and what a violent maelstrom of destruction and horror your inner soul must be.[38]

Horror at the degeneration of relationship expressed in the letter is in the novel transmuted into a judgment.

These are characters immersed in the river of dissolution. As further examples of the novel's disintegrative movement, we remember that physical death is an almost continuous presence in *Women in Love*. There is the drowning of Diana Crich, which recalls Gerald's early accidental killing of his brother; the slow dying of Thomas Crich, which colors the middle episodes of the narrative; the death of Gerald himself. We are aware, too, of the lurking menace of death in Birkin, whose health is evidently precarious. Before she pledges herself to Birkin, Ursula too finds her body beginning to absorb the poison of her spirit's despair; for it was Lawrence's belief that "the body is only one of the manifestations of the spirit, the transmutation of the integral spirit is the transmutation of the physical body as well" (*WIL*, p. 184).

In Lawrence the river of dissolution and the river of life often run mingled. I have discussed his double sense of Birkin and Ursula, as not wholly positive forces; his sympathy for Gudrun and Gerald, particularly Gudrun; and his appreciation of the grotesque Loerke—although Loerke is seen much more from the outside, as a figure of caricature. I have argued that Lawrence's feeling for Breadalby is like that of his characters, painfully mixed: its gracious beauty and the unhurried grace of the aristocratic way of life have real attraction; and yet the tradition of a static domination has become stale, unproductive of new meetings.

There are other such ambivalent judgments within the texture of the novel. These are admirably discussed in Colin Clarke's *River of Dissolution.*[39] Clarke describes, for instance, the way in which the chapter "Coal Dust" has such mingled effect. Clearly we are to see Beldover as ugly, uncreated, its inhabitants the lost denizens of an underworld. Yet the hellish landscape is powerfully attractive, as are the people of the mining town. As Gudrun and Ursula walk towards the colliery district at sunset, a narcotic glamor invests the scene, not unlike the narcotic underworld of the Pompadour, as described in "Crême de Menthe."

> The heavy gold glamour of approaching sunset lay over all the colliery district, and the ugliness overlaid with beauty was like a narcotic to the senses. On the roads silted with black dust, the rich light fell more warmly, more heavily, over all the amorphous squalor a kind of magic was cast, from the glowing close of day (*WIL,* p. 107).

The "voluptuous resonance of darkness" that Gudrun senses in the miners has a profound attraction for Lawrence, who, from childhood pulled between the light and the dark, finds Pluto a powerful tutelary spirit.

Lawrence was bound to these miners by the deepest ties; these are the familiar associates of his childhood. In December 1915, just before beginning work on *Women in Love,* he writes of the miners of Derbyshire:

> These men are passionate enough, sensuous, dark—God, how all my boyhood comes back— so violent, so dark, the mind always dark and without understanding, the senses violently active. It makes me sad beyond words. These men, whom I love so much—and the life has such a power over me—they *understand* mentally so horribly: only industrialism, only wages and money and machinery.

He fights his love for them: "One must conquer them also—think beyond them, know beyond them, act beyond them."[40] The nostalgia ascribed to Gudrun is Lawrence's also.

In the same way Birkin's passionate longing for isolation as he rolls alone in the wet vegetation is Lawrence's own; yet he fights it, through the judgment of *Women in Love* and in such short stories as "The Man Who Loved Islands" and "The Man Who Died." Hermione, too, is in Lawrence, and is thus an enemy worth fighting. Her sense of insufficiency to herself and her need for Birkin are close to the feelings expressed by Lawrence in Frieda's absence, as they find their way into such poems as "Humiliation" and "Mutilation" in the

volume *Look! We Have Come Through.*[41] I have mentioned the sympathy
with which Lawrence creates Gudrun; he finds much beauty also in Minette
and in the sculpture that seems to represent her, conveying, according to
Birkin, "a complete truth": the perfect expression of an understanding through
the senses.[42]

The bright river of life and the dark waters of corruption swirl ineluctably
together. In fact, Colin Clarke develops the thesis that in *Women in Love* they
are inextricably mingled within the experience of the novel. "The strategy is
directed *throughout* to affirming but also calling in question (often
simultaneously) the dichotomies of decadence and growth, purity and
degradation, the paradisal and demonic."[43] Is this really true in the novel, or
does the reader find that Lawrence does make a choice? He declares in "The
Reality of Peace" that "creation is primal, corruption is only a consequence";
do we find this also revealed, beyond assertion, in the more complex statement
of the novel?

For Lawrence the dialectic of creation and sundering is the basis of
productive action. Insight, as noted previously, is a passing revelation, a
moment of abiding importance that is incarnate only within the changing
instant. Since this is a moment in time, it is caught between the waves of
gathering together and sundering, of separation and renewal.

> It is that which comes when night clashes on day, the rainbow, the yellow and rose and blue
> and purple of dawn and sunset, which leaps out of the breaking of light upon darkness, of
> darkness upon light, absolute beyond day or night; the rainbow, the iridescence which is
> darkness at once and light, the two-in-one; the crown that binds them both.[44]

And so, too, with the process of human life.

> While we live, we are balanced between the flux of life and the flux of death. All the while
> our bodies are being composed and decomposed. But while every man fully lives, all the time
> the two streams keep fusing into the third reality, of real creation. Every new gesture, every
> fresh smile of a child is a new emergence into creative being: a glimpse of the Holy Ghost....
> And each year the blossoming is different: from the delicate blue speedwells of childhood to
> the equally delicate, frail farewell flowers of old age: through all the poppies and sunflowers:
> year after year of difference.[45]

Therefore, part of the power of *Women in Love* is in its mingling of the two
streams, in the image of creation that takes account of the reality of
destruction. The book is forged in the world of experience by an imagination
possessed by visionary hope.

For Lawrence there is beauty in submission to the movement of sundering
in its right temporal relation to that of life, a beauty which is the subject of the
poem "Beautiful Old Age" and of the following comment in "The Crown":

And the still clear look on an old face, and the stillness of old, withered hands, which have gathered the long repose of autumn, this is the purity of the two streams consummated, and the bloom, like autumn crocuses, of age.[46]

It is the static, impermeable state of egoism that is death; the way of life represented by Hermione, Thomas Crich, and Palmer is a greater falsity than is the energy, albeit destructive energy, of Gerald Crich, Gudrun, Loerke. Moreover, destruction may itself be creative, as—again in right temporal relation to its opposing tendency—it bursts the outworn forms, the carapaces of habit; for all renewal involves death. Birkin's revolutionary sentiments as outlined in the train to Gerald echo Lawrence's in "The Crown" and in the letters of this time; and a similar parallel obtains between Birkin's and Lawrence's struggle for a new life, in a different place, clear of the old people.

The energizing spirit of destruction, bursting old forms, is a creative force in writing as in living. For Lawrence, the plot of his novel, as a breaking through to a new kind of relationship between two people, is analogous to—is indeed part of the same process as—the need of the novelist to forge a new formal relationship between his imaginative perception and the material world.

The sundering wave is as necessary to life as the creative. Yet Lawrence's profession of faith is that the two waves are not equally original: "creation is primal and original, corruption is only a consequence."[47] This is a belief central to "The Reality of Peace" and to "The Crown," and is, in my view, woven into the texture of the novel, creating what is finally a statement of hope.

Our culture is fulfilled in disintegration. In "The Crown" Lawrence describes this process as being the analytic, separating habit of thought which in *Women in Love* he represents in the images of the industrial empire of the Criches, the sexual meeting of Gerald and Gudrun, the ambiance of Breadalby, and avant-garde Bohemia. But, he adds in "The Crown,"

If we have our fill of destruction, then we shall turn again to creation. We shall need to live again, and live hard, for once our great civilized form is broken, and we are at last born into the open sky, we shall have a whole new universe to grow up into, and to find relations with.[48]

It is in new relationship, the perception of a quickened world, that we will have our renewal.

If we are to break through, it must be in the strength of life bubbling inside us. The chicken does not break the shell out of animosity against the shell. It bursts out in its blind desire to move under a greater heavens.[49]

In "The Crown" Lawrence stands with Ursula: the new life grows "out of us," not "after us."

In "The Reality of Peace" Lawrence says that the state of spring is primal. In *Women in Love* spring is a frequent image, nourishing our sense of the growing relationship between Birkin and Ursula. The action begins in early spring; Birkin first notices Ursula amid an atmosphere of growth, as her class studies the early catkins; Ursula's self-development is described often in terms of a growing shoot, a budding flower. At the end of the novel she turns away from the abstract inhumanity of Loerke's explanation of his art; in the eternal frozen snow of the mountains she thinks of an alternative.

> Now suddenly, as by a miracle she remembered that away beyond, below her, lay the dark fruitful earth, that towards the south there were stretches of land dark with orange trees and cypress, grey with olives, that ilex trees lifted wonderful plumy tufts in shadow against a blue sky.... She wanted to see the dark earth, to smell its earthy fecundity, to see the patient wintry vegetation, to feel the sunshine touch a response in the buds (*WIL,* p. 425).

It is such organic connection that Birkin seeks with Ursula. A flower that blossoms is dependent on earth, sun, and rain; but it is itself an irreplaceable reality—as even "the prickly sow-thistle I have just pulled up *is,* for the first time in all time."[50] So Birkin sees that he and Ursula each must retain individuality and yet accept "the obligation of permanent connection with others and with the other" (*WIL,* p. 247). Paradoxically, this involves dying, a losing of the self to find the self; or, perhaps, the dissolution of the walled ego to discover the open self. "I deliver *myself* over to the unknown, in coming to you, I am without reserves or defences..." (*WIl,* p. 138).

As in the relationships described in *The Rainbow,* Birkin sees such confrontation as a moving into the unknown; for the other is not oneself, is not a mirror image, but ineluctably different. This belief is central to Lawrence's understanding of a person's connection with the world—not just in human relationships, though it is seen in most essential form in the sexual union between man and woman. Thus Birkin criticizes Hermione for possessing everything as a mirror image of herself, and she for her part is frustrated and angry when she finds Birkin copying a painting of Chinese geese, not in order to make something of his own but to understand the goose in its alien being. After the constricting possessiveness of Breadalby, Birkin rejoices in the subtle freshness of wet trees and grasses which are independent of any meaning assigned by his consciousness. The Italian Contessa notices that as Birkin dances, "he is not a man, he is a chameleon, a creature of change" (*WIL,* p. 85). Others notice a similar fluid insouciance, which is in contrast to Gerald's tight grasp of his consciousness: "Gerald could never fly away from himself, in real indifferent gaiety. He had a clog, a sort of monomania" (*WIL,* p. 199).

In human relationship, therefore, there is a nonpersonal dimension, which is that, too, of a person's relatedness to the nonhuman world; man must see that he is not of primary importance. This is Birkin's final insouciance:

Well, if mankind is destroyed, if our race is destroyed like Sodom, and there is this beautiful evening with the luminous land and trees, I am satisfied. That which informs it all is there, and can never be lost (*WIL,* p. 52).[51]

I have so far discussed the hope of Birkin, the kind of relationship desired in the novel, mainly through statements of description or intent. However, it is not in statement or argument that Lawrence's understanding of such relatedness is most satisfactorily explored, but in the novel's symbolic scenes: the argument is substantiated, the statements proved, through narrative images.

One night Ursula wanders down to Willey Water, absorbed in angry repudiation of Birkin, friends, family—hard and brilliant like the moon that she presently sees rising among the trees. Then she notices a shadowy figure moving by the water: it is Birkin, talking to himself, and cursing the moon's reflection as the image of Ursula, "the accursed Syria Dea," the earth mother who draws all to herself. He begins throwing stones at the reflection in the water, trying in frenzy to destroy the moon from the face of the lake. Shattering its image he casts stone after stone, but ever the moon reforms itself in broken waves, a center remains quivering and rocking but whole. At last he succeeds in shattering the surface of the pond with such violence the image has become only a dance of turbulent splintered fragments upon the water; the night rocks with the noise; shadow and light appear here and there, chaotic. Birkin is satisfied, Ursula shattered. "She felt she had fallen to the ground and was spilled out like water on the earth." Yet the light begins once more to gather itself, persistently reforming, until "a ragged rose, a distorted, frayed moon was shaking upon the water again, re-asserted, renewed, trying to recover from its convulsion, to get over the disfigurement and the agitation, to be whole and composed, at peace" (*WIL,* p. 240). Ursula goes to join Birkin by the water's edge.

The dialogue between Birkin and Ursula is an extension of the fight over what he sees as a false idea of connection, her will to possess him. He has destroyed that spirit of repudiation in her; yet her essential self forms invisibly again, whole, composed, at peace. Their subsequent verbal dialogue and their drawing together are affected by this dialogue of gesture.

But this is only a part of it. More striking is the extraordinary power of the scene as a real battle between Birkin, using his utmost force to destroy the moon's reflection on the water, and the persistent, indomitable light which insists, as a living creature, on the coherence of its being. From the beginning of the episode Ursula is cowed by the domination of the moon, as it looks down on her, illuminating the open landscape, mercilessly reflecting Ursula's own repudiation of will, which now seeks the shadow of receptive dialogue. So she makes for the wood, where the moon is no longer apparent; until she notices that it rides high and calm in the dark water, once more a perfect, an intimidating presence. As Birkin throws stones at the moon's reflection, he seems not to be indulging a whimsical fancy but fighting a real antagonist.

> The furthest waves of light, fleeing out, seemed to be clamouring against the shore for escape, the waves of darkness came in heavily, running under towards the centre. But at the centre, the heart of all, was still a vivid, incandescent quivering of a white moon not quite destroyed, a white body of fire writhing and striving and not even now broke open, not yet violated. It seemed to be drawing itself together with strange, violent pangs, in blind effort (*WIL*, p. 239).

There is uncanny drama in the event, affecting the reader as more than the subjective expression of anger on the part of Birkin.

A similar image in Conrad's *Lord Jim* points up the difference in effect of such description in the two writers. Marlow describes a visit to Jim in Patusan, during which they watch the moon rise behind two hills.

> On the third day after the full, the moon . . . rose exactly behind these hills, its diffused light at first throwing the two masses into intensely black relief, and then the nearly perfect disc, glowing ruddily, appeared, gliding upwards between the sides of the chasm, till it floated away above the summits, as if escaping from a yawning grave in gentle triumph. "Wonderful effect," said Jim by my side. "Worth seeing. Is it not?"

Conrad's natural world is a *paysage moralisé;* here the landscape is created in the form of Jim's triumph—as Marlow himself suggests: "He had regulated so many things in Patusan—things that would have appeared as much beyond his control as the motions of the moon and the stars."[52]

For Conrad the natural world is alien to man—inscrutable, malevolent to his designs, possessing its own unsearchable life. Connection is established by the creative act of will, as in the image of the moon rising in the reflection of Jim's proud imagination. Thus a more objective description, in an earlier passage, must be metaphoric: the connection is established through metaphor that exhibits difference rather than intrinsic connection. The moon is "like a slender shaving thrown up from a bar of gold"; the stars seem "to shed upon the earth the assurance of everlasting security."[53]

Lawrence's moon is not merely an analogical image describing Birkin's hostility, but exhibits, as it seems, an authentic resistance, beyond anthropomorphism. There are two equivalent and parallel forms of reality: the moon in her chill and brilliant domination of the night, Ursula in her cold rejection of human beings; the moon shattered, the waves settling, the image reforming, and Ursula persisting in the steadiness of her inviolable self. Birkin finds that he is unable to impose himself finally on the incandescent light, that it is not his to destroy, that Ursula's self is not his to impose himself on. In the total event the parts, though distinguishable, are inseparable: wood, water, and moon being no less living than man and girl.

This is the revelation that Lawrence speaks of in "The Crown," in which isolated phenomena form themselves into the momentary coherence of lively connection.

> Our universe is not much more than a mannerism with us now. If we break through, we shall find, that man is not man, as he seems to be, nor woman woman. The present seeming is a ridiculous travesty. And even the sun is not the sun as it appears to be. It is something tingling with magnificence.
>
> And then starts the one glorious activity of man: the getting himself into a new relationship with a new heaven and a new earth.[54]

It remains a question whether such apocalypse is a revelation within the heightened imagination of the participants of the action—the reader included, drawn by the power of the symbol—or is, as Lawrence would maintain, a self-substantiating reality, a transpersonal apocalypse. "What makes life good to me," Lawrence declares,

> is the sense that, even if I am sick and ill, I am alive, alive to the depths of my soul, and in touch somewhere in touch with the vivid life of the cosmos. Somehow my life draws strength from the depths of the universe, from the depths among the stars, from the great "world." Out of the great world comes my strength and my reassurance. One could say "God," but the word "God" is somehow tainted. But there *is* a flame or a Life Everlasting wreathing through the cosmos for ever and giving us our renewal, once we can get in touch with it.[55]

Another early meeting between Birkin and Ursula illustrates further such *apokalypsis,* a revelation to character and reader of an accord that enwraps the human participants yet does not appear limited to their personal activities. In "An Island" Ursula has been arguing with Birkin, denying his end-of-the-world predictions, insisting on a future of human possibility. Her words are given life by a small important action which then takes place. Birkin drops a series of daisy stems into the water, watches them drift downstream in bright convoy, their white flowers open and radiant on the dark water. Ursula watches them, and watches Birkin, who is absorbed in their passage "with bright, absolved eyes." A "strange feeling" possesses her, as if "something were taking place." But it is all "intangible" (*WIL,* 123). Birkin is at this moment a part of the total event, in such living connection that it is as if he were himself the human counterpart of the daisy flotilla whose "gay bright candour" moves Ursula almost to tears. These flowers are indeed part of the "pure creation" of which Birkin has just been speaking, the "world of trees and grass and birds" that do not depend on man. But Ursula is right too, for the power of the moment is in the scene as an inclusive total event: the man and girl watching, as well as the daisies drifting; the girl seeing, without articulating this, the man crouching on the water's edge absorbed, in human aspect a part of the revelation of innocence. To reduce it even more crudely—for this is something that we sense powerfully, yet within the image and, therefore elusively—Birkin is at this moment a part of the "pure creation."

Again, how far the daisies' candor depends on the man's seeing it as such, how far their brightness illuminates him, is a matter for a Wallace Stevens to write of. For Lawrence, as I have said, daisies, like "grass and hares and adders," live freely in glamorous independence of man, connected with him in an eternally changing process that he variously attributes to the "life flame," the "Holy Spirit," or—sometimes, hesitantly—"God."

One of the triumphs of *Women in Love* is that the search for a relation of commitment which will yet leave each lover free within his and her integral being takes place through action that both articulates this love and persuades us of it through its illustration in alternative mode. In the scenes which I have discussed, the apocalypse, the revelation of life which is discovered by the two in their love for each other, is revealed to them—and to the reader—through events which themselves embody such relationship: living connection is found between wood, girl, water, man, yet each entity possesses its own individuality. At such moments the world manifests itself through an erotic interchange, which has its human incarnation in the love of Birkin and Ursula. In loving they are part of a natural dialogue whose various revelations are for the writer the means by which he explores the growth of human love.

Sometimes this heightened perception occurs as the revelation of death. In the snow scene of the final chapters of the novel, Lawrence evokes magnificently a frozen world, both outer and inner; for Gerald finds his final destination on the icy slope of the mountain, which is the outer counterpart of his cold isolation of spirit and the lapse of his hope.[56] The manner of his death seems to be the further unfolding of an inner process, and so has for the reader the power less of authorial contrivance than of inevitable consummation. Before his death he has been identified specifically with the cold brilliance of the scene.

> The first days passed in an ecstacy of physical motion, sleighing, ski-ing, skating, moving in an intensity of speed and white light that surpassed life itself, and carried the souls of the human beings beyond into an inhuman abstraction of velocity and weight and eternal frozen snow (*WIL,* p. 411).

Gerald is at one with this motion, "his muscles elastic in a perfect, soaring trajectory, his body projected in pure flight, mindless, soulless, whirling along one perfect line of force" (*WIL,* pp. 411-12). Ursula, however, finds that only her love for Birkin warms her in this "cold, eternal place," and that without him it would, as she says, "kill the quick of my life" (*WIL,* p. 398). Before long she finds that her spirit is bruised by the ice-bound place; they must move south, to the soft earth, the breaking shoots. But Gerald is in his element, as he had been in an earlier scene, diving in Willey Water. "He must stay up there in the snow forever. He had been happy by himself, high up there alone, travelling swiftly on skis, taking far flights, and skimming past the dark rocks veined with brilliant snow." When he returns he is "isolated as if there were a vacuum round his heart, or a sheath of pure ice" (*WIL,* pp. 451-52).

In Gerald's death Birkin finds manifested the frozen life that has been his friend's. He looks at the icy body, the "cold, mute, material face," and that face sends "a shaft like ice through the heart of the living man" (*WIL,* p. 471). The isolation of heart which was Gerald's denial of Birkin and of any relationship in faith has its counterpart in the inaccessible frozen cliff and snow waste where he dies.

> But the cradle of snow ran on to the eternal closing-in, where the walls of snow and rock rose impenetrable, and the mountain peaks above were in heaven immediate. This was the centre, the knot, the navel of the world, where the earth belonged to the skies, pure, unapproachable, impassable (*WIL,* p. 391).

To this evocation of the inner and outer landscape of death the reader makes a double response: aware of the frozen scene, he yet finds a counter tendency which is the excitement of the discovery of such interpenetration of human and nonhuman worlds; the creative power of the image denies Gerald's search for isolation.[57]

Gerald, in the final snow episode of the novel, achieves mythic stature, through identification with the landscape itself: his snow death enacts the ritual that is myth's other mode. Not only in this scene, however, but elsewhere in the book as well, such "conventionalizing" ritual action is evident. Hitherto I have discussed *Women in Love* in its realistic aspect as a pyschological narrative and in its parabolic aspect as an apocalyptic drama. Now I should like to turn to what is a further dimension of the parabolic, the ritual nature of the novel.

John Vickery, in a useful documentation of the connections between Lawrence's writing and Frazer's *Golden Bough,* points out with numerous examples from the fiction that specific ritual actions described by Frazer are employed within the course of Lawrence's narrative.[58] It is clear, of course, that many scenes in *Women in Love* carry a ritual charge: the moon scene I have discussed, that in which Birkin rolls in the wet vegetation, Gudrun's dance before the cattle, the transmogrifying of the rabbit into demonic beast. I have not the space to discuss these scenes; but there is one aspect of ritual narrative which is especially pertinent to my theme.

As I said in my introduction, Lawrence had no patience with the ethics implied in the book of Revelation. He preferred to read the Apocalypse as the narrative of a pagan initiation ritual layered with Christian accretions, the rites of an Eastern Mediterranean goddess such as Artemis or Cybele. As Lawrence presents the narrative, the seven seals that are opened in the Christian book of

Revelation were originally the seven centers of bodily consciousness; the four horsemen, the four natures of man, much as in medieval physiology. The body of the initiate must die, to be reborn to the mysteries of the goddess, his mystic "third eye" now opened.[59]

The account of the Woman Clothed with the Sun, brief as it is in the book of Revelation, is for Lawrence the most primitive and essential part of the Apocalypse: "And there appeared a great wonder in heaven; a woman clothed with the sun, and the moon under her feet, and upon her head a crown of twelve stars:..." (Revelation 12:1). Of this figure Lawrence says:

> She has brought into the Bible what it lacked before: the great cosmic Mother robed and splendid, but persecuted. And she is, of course, essential to the scheme of power and splendour, which must have a queen: unlike the religions of renunciation, which are womanless.[60]

According to Lawrence, the Great Whore of Babylon is the moralistic delineation by later apocalyptists of the Woman Clothed with the Sun, "the Magna Mater in malefic aspect."[61]

Woman in Love is a story of initiation in which the novice is born to a new reality. Lawrence's account of the love of Birkin and Ursula has repeated moments of such initiatory plot: firstly, in the revelations of life, as outlined in my discussion earlier; secondly, in more direct account by the author of the lovers' sense of rebirth to each other. Lawrence describes Ursula's understanding of her committedness to Birkin, early in their friendship, as follows: "It was a fight to the death between them—or to new life: though in what the conflict lay, no one could say" (*WIL*, p. 135). In the events which follow Diana's drowning, after Ursula and Birkin have met in passionate lovemaking, he leaves her "satisfied and shattered, fulfilled and destroyed." As they drive later into the country it seems to Birkin that their love has brought him to new birth.

> He seemed to be conscious all over, all his body awake with a simple, glimmering awareness, as if he had just come awake, like a thing that is born, like a bird when it comes out of an egg, into a new universe (*WIL*, p. 303).

So for Ursula, as if she were an initiate seeing with the third eye, her lover is transfigured.

> New eyes were opened in her soul. She saw a strange creature from another world, in him. It was as if she were enchanted, and everything were metamorphosed. She recalled again the old magic of the Book of Genesis, where the sons of God saw the daughters of men, that they were fair (*WIL*, p. 304).

Their love is consummated—and it seems that this is the first full consummation—in Sherwood Forest, where they are attended by natural witnesses, as at a ritual sacred marriage.

> She saw that they were running among trees—great old trees with dying bracken undergrowth. The palish, gnarled trunks showed ghostly, and like old priests in the hovering distance, the fern rose magical and mysterious. . . . There were faint sounds from the wood, but no disturbance, no possible disturbance, the world was under a strange ban, a new mystery had surpervened (*WIL,* p. 312).

As to the "palpable revelation of mystic otherness," of which the novelist speaks later in the scene, the narrative is clearly inadequate here—probably inevitably so, considering the incommunicability of the subject in verbal terms. But the scene is carried by the power of the earlier description of the drive out of town, through the countryside, early evening, the entrance to the forest.

In another scene, one that seems to be parallel to this consummation of their love in the sacred grove, the writer describes the channel crossing at night, as a dropping away from the old life, a wonderful evocation of death and rebirth.

> They seemed to fall away into the profound darkness. There was no sky, no earth, only one unbroken darkness, into which, with a soft, sleeping motion, they seemed to fall like one closed seed of life falling through dark, fathomless space (*WIL,* p. 378).

The whole scene forms both a sexual and sensual image, as well as an image of the ritual of initiation.

That Lawrence invested Ursula with the mystic attributes of the Woman Clothed with the Sun is evident from the imagery by means of which he describes her, as she seems to Birkin, in his capacity of initiate into the mysteries of the goddess. I have mentioned that she is throughout connected with images of budding and growth, seen as a newly opened flower. But more important to her delineation as the Woman Clothed with the Sun is the frequency with which she is described as appearing to Birkin enwrapped with the golden light of the goddess. In "An Island" he sees

> her face strangely enkindled, as if suffused from within by a powerful sweet fire. His soul was arrested in wonder. She was enkindled in her own living fire. Arrested in wonder and in pure, perfect attraction, he moved towards her. She sat like a strange queen, almost supernatural in her glowing smiling richness (*WIL,* p. 122).

As she sits alone (in the chapter called "Sunday Morning") contemplating her future life, Birkin interrupts her reflections. She seems to him tranfused with light, as if she were a supernatural being.

> He looked at her and wondered at the luminous delicacy of her beauty, and the wide shining
> of her eyes. He watched from a distance, with wonder in his heart, she seemed transfigured
> with light (*WIL,* p. 186).

Thus it is that when he declares his love for her it is in the figure of an aureole of light.

> And being silent, he remembered the beauty of her eyes, which were sometimes filled with
> light, like spring, suffused with wonderful promise. So he said to her, slowly with difficulty.
> "There is a golden light in you, which I wish you would give me." It was as if he had been
> thinking of this for some time (*WIL,* p. 241).

In this example the power of the biblical image meets the impulse from which such an image arose: the sense of an ever-creating nature, an eternally renewed spring. Ursula is here the goddess of the river of life, the Mary of Fra Angelico's painting, a rose "warm and flamy" opposed to the lily of corruption, and the representative of hope in a time of destruction. Lawrence is perhaps remembering his portrait of Ursula when he describes the woman of the book of Revelation as "the woman of the cosmos wrapped in her warm gleam like the sun."[62]

The figure of the Woman Clothed with the Sun stands at the center of the initiation narrative that is Lawrence's reading of the apocalyptic story in the book of Revelation. In Jung's *Answer to Job* she represents also the divine Sophia who unites with Yahweh in the *hieros gamos* and the Bride, the redeemed for whom Christ is the Bridegroom, in the New Testament Apocalypse. As goddess and female participant in that hierogamy suggested, perhaps, in Birkin's "sort of ultimate marriage," Ursula is certainly delineated as I have described; she is seen by Birkin as "something translucent and simple, like a radiant, shining flower that moment unfolded in primal blessedness" (*WIL,* p. 360). In later fiction Lawrence further develops the mythical aspect of the woman in marriage; my discussion of *The Plumed Serpent, The Man Who Died,* and *Lady Chatterley's Lover* will treat of this more fully.

In the book of Revelation the final redemption in which the apocalyptist envisions a renewed Paradise is announced through images of marriage: "the marriage of the Lamb," and "new Jerusalem, coming down from God out of heaven, prepared as a bride adorned for her husband" (Revelation 19:7; 21:2). Gudrun and Gerald mockingly refer to echoes of such imagery in some of Birkin's assertions about marriage. Birkin believes, says Gudrun:

> "that a man and wife can go further than any other two beings. . . . They can know each other,
> heavenly and hellish, but particularly hellish, so perfectly that they go beyond heaven and
> hell—into—there it all breaks down—into nowhere."
> "Into Paradise, he says," laughed Gerald (*WIL,* p. 282).

Their ironic deprecation, however, does not discredit Birkin's real belief.

Yet this is no eternal Paradise, as it is in the book of Revelation, but one found in glimpses, and in the warmth of attraction that the ebb of repudiation does not destroy. It incorporates the destruction brought about through isolation and strife and the history of past failure. Paradise, the full moment, the *apokalypsis,* is continually lost and refound. Thus, though the novel ends in sadness, there is no doubt of the reality of the profound love of Birkin and Ursula for each other. Such love is the more powerful and the more moving since it is so hard won, and therefore perilous. It needs only a single spark of faith, says Lawrence, to enkindle the fire of conversion. So Birkin, deep in despair at his own and his society's rage for destruction, yet finds in himself that one spark, like a single seed:

> Her soul was new, undefined and glimmering with the unseen. And his soul was dark and gloomy, it had only one grain of living hope, like a grain of mustard seed. But this one living grain in him matched the perfect youth in her.

So he is moved to "pure hope, like a man who is born again to a wonderful, lively hope far exceeding the bounds of death" (*WIL,* p. 361).

4

The Plumed Serpent: Visitation of Pan or *Deus ex Machina?*

Through his love for Ursula, Birkin finds the means for self-renewal in the midst of a society dying of spiritual inanition. In *Apocalypse,* his counterpart, the novice whom Lawrence hypothesizes as undergoing the ritual adumbrated in the book of Revelation, dies a psychic death and is reborn a new man. As a sign that he has died in the old body he is "sealed in the forehead like a Hindu monk." The seal is the third eye, what Lawrence calls the "mystic eye" of the twice-born, which sees through its former world to the reality within.[1]

The man who was at least the immediate cause of Lawrence's speculations on the nature of the apocalypse was the occultist Frederick Carter, mentioned earlier. The Lawrences visited Carter in 1923 at his Shropshire home in order to discuss the idea of apocalypse. As a result of this meeting, Lawrence wrote an introduction to Carter's book, which was then in manuscript form, entitled *The Dragon of the Apocalypse.* Lawrence soon afterwards fictionalized Carter— rather unpleasantly (and ungratefully)—as the Cartwright of "St. Mawr," an artist interested in astrology and the occult, an eccentric who is an uneasy member of the staid village community in which he has chosen to settle. He interests Lou Witt, however, when he delivers a disquisition on the goat-Pan, whom he curiously resembles.

But what, asks Lou, was the original form of Pan, before his devolution into a lascivious goat-satyr? Cartwright describes the original Pan as the hidden *theos* which is present within a natural object for the observer able to perceive it. Pan was the immanent Cause.

> "He was Pan. All: what you see when you see in full. In the daytime you see the thing. But if your third eye is open, which sees only the things that can't be seen, you may see Pan within the thing, hidden: you may see with your third eye, which is darkness."[2]

The conversation between Cartwright and Lou is fairly brief, but the image of Pan serves to evoke a quality of perception that is extensively, if implicitly, explored in "St. Mawr" and that, variously described, expresses a belief central to Lawrence's vision.

Nor is the icon of Pan confined to "St. Mawr." In 1924 Lawrence wrote a short essay out of his experience in New Mexico entitled "Pan in America." He develops in this essay the contrast between a pre-modern sense of the necessity for finding and maintaining connection with the strange and different life of the nonhuman world and what he sees as modern man's denial of the reality of this imperative.

Modern man resists the Pan within him, preferring to conquer his environment rather than live in cooperation with it. But in the New Mexico of Indian culture, Lawrence believed, the ancient power of Pan still lurks. It is apparent in the pine tree overshadowing Lawrence's cabin:

> It vibrates its presence into my soul, and I am with Pan. I think no man could live near a pine tree and remain quite suave and supple and compliant. Something fierce and bristling is communicated. The piny sweetness is rousing and defiant, like turpentine, the noise of the needles is keen with aeons of sharpness. In the volleys of wind from the western desert, the tree hisses and resists. It does not lean eastward at all. It resists with a vast force of resistance, from within itself, and its column is a ribbed, magnificent assertion.[3]

When Ramón tries to convince Kate, in *The Plumed Serpent*, of the necessity of their presenting themselves as avatars of the former gods of the Aztecs, Kate balks at the idea of representing, indeed in some sense becoming, the First Woman of Itzpapalotl. But Ramón believes in the power of the gods incarnate as living icons for the people:

> "There must be manifestations. We *must* change back to the vision of the living cosmos; we *must*.... I accept the *must* from the oldest Pan in my soul, and from the newest *me*."[4]

The religion of Quetzalcoatl attempts to revitalize the Pan power among the Mexican people, and Kate in marrying Cipriano marries less an individual—so goes the intention, at least—than a potent embodiment of the "god-demon" Pan, their marriage thus enacting a hierogamy that exemplifies the right organization of energy.

It is apparent, therefore, that the image of Pan and that of the third eye at this time became another means for the writer of embodying a desired and elusive sense of vitality. Lawrence himself became increasingly aware of the centrality of this vision to his own thinking, and more urgently, indeed desperately, sought to proclaim what he perceived as the only vital attitude to the world in the face of a society bent on fragmentation. Pan has power to release Narcissus from his reflexive gaze. Accordingly, that sense of reality which, till the war, had formed the endoskeleton of his work now assumed more of the nature of an exoskeleton. *Fantasia of the Unconscious, Aaron's Rod,* "St. Mawr," *The Plumed Serpent, Lady Chatterley's Lover, The Man Who Died, Apocalypse*—as well as many of the later poems—all exhibit an avowed preoccupation with the question of man's neglected attunement to the body of the world.

In *Aaron's Rod*, Aaron breaks out of a confining marriage to wander in search of a way of life or a person who will speak to his wandering, to the vagrant self that has been developing within him. Among the various individuals whom he encounters in his confused pilgrimage, only Lilly seems to have found a satisfying way to be in the world; Aaron is as much intrigued by Lilly's insouciance as by his intent presence.

> Aaron looked at Lilly, and saw the same odd, distant look on his face as on the face of some animal when it lies awake and alert, yet perfectly at one with its surroundings. It was something quite different from happiness: an alert enjoyment of rest, an intense and satisfying sense of centrality. As a dog when it basks in the sun with one eye open and winking: or a rabbit quite still and wide-eyed, with a faintly-twitching nose.[5]

Following Lilly's example, Aaron journeys to Italy and there discovers a new kind of response in himself: "He felt like a man who knows it is time to wake up, and who doesn't want to wake up, to face the responsibility of another sort of day."[6]

Lawrence, intent like Lilly on coming into possession of his own soul and believing that "a new place brings out a new thing in a man," was driven to Italy, to Ceylon, Australia, New Mexico, Mexico, partly in desperation, partly in the faith of Abraham, who "when he was called to go out into a place which he should after receive for an inheritance obeyed; and he went out, not knowing whither he went" (Hebrews 11).

And it seemed that in New Mexico Lawrence found the accord that had been lost in Europe. "In the magnificent fierce morning of New Mexico one sprang awake, a new part of the soul woke up suddenly, and the old world gave way to a new."[7] Here was the reality that he had sought: "I had looked all over the world for something that would strike me as religious."[8] He had found this awesome reality not only in the mountain ranges, the trees, and skies of New Mexico, but also in the pueblos, among the presences and rituals of the Indians as they remained, though diminished from their former numbers and cultural strength. Therefore his discussion of an individual's renewal would be likely to turn more intensely than before on the necessity for cultural change: ritual as the group expression of belief.

So it is that whereas apocalypse in *The Rainbow* and in *Women in Love* is an event of unexpected and momentary power occurring within and between individuals, in *The Plumed Serpent* apocalyptic conversion is formalized into ritual: deliberate, lengthy, and exemplary.

The novice whose conversion is described in the course of *The Plumed Serpent* is Kate Leslie, who realizes that in coming from Ireland to Mexico she has traversed a divide, has "crossed the great water" spiritually as well as geographically.[9] At the midpoint of her life, she has experienced the satisfactions of sexual love, marriage, and motherhood, and she remains in search. She sees her culture as emotionally exhausted; the old ideal of love is now hypocritically practiced, for the ground of its praxis has been lost: the Christian ethic remains only as the shell surrounding a desiccated spirituality.

As I have already pointed out, Lawrence believed in God as a perennially changing force. Whoever would search for this God must "listen to the dark hound of heaven, and start off into the dark of the unknown."[10] Lawrence articulates with increasing directness a belief in God, but in a God whose mode changes continually, just as the act of attention that is poetry finds itself in the fleeting moment, as Paradise is the motion of change, as love is traveling. Always Lawrence distrusts the static, the formed; he prefers to see the running stream, the moment of the poppy's scarlet blossoming, the hare's leap in the moonlight, the woman, self-collected, turning toward the light of the lamp. "The whole tide of all life and all time suddenly heaves, and appears before us as an apparition, a revelation." This was the quarrel he had with Brewster regarding Nirvana—as he imperfectly understood it, or was given to understand it by Brewster. Nirvana for Lawrence is the open moment, terra incognita. And what interests Lawrence in the novel is the play of life in motion; the task of the novelist is to be aware continually of the "myriad sun in chaos."

Kate finds herself weary of what she sees as Christianity's enervated ethic and longs for a new spirituality. "Gods die with men who have conceived them. But the god-stuff roars eternally, like the sea, with too vast a sound to be heard" (*PS*, p. 63). She seeks the unfolding of a central peace within herself, that self-collectedness that Lawrence called wisdom—speechless, yet tuned to the pulse of the living world. She comes to Mexico, uprooting herself from children, parents, friends. Although she finds the place repellent, squalid, there is in its atmosphere a certain power, a certain magnetism that intrigues her.

The first two episodes of the novel detail examples of her ambivalent sense of the country, and provide images of that which she wishes to cast off. The first is the occasion of the bullfight, a squalid and petty event that leaves her disgusted with Mexico and disillusioned with her American companions who watch the affair with determined zest. In both Mexican and American she perceives a lust for sensationalism of a degrading kind. The subtle and complex battle of wills between bull and horse and man has degenerated into a pitiful charade between the bull, no longer that fiery "mithraic beast" of myth but a bemused creature stumbling about the enclosure, and the matador who goads him at intervals, an obese and effeminate charlatan with none of the pride of the bull's wary opponent. As for the horse, the bull's spirited and powerful enemy, this is an enfeebled nag, half dead before the fight. "O shades of Don Quixote! O four Spanish horsemen of the Apocalypse!" (*PS*, p. 16).

Thus a contest of elemental opposition is reduced to a petty display of cowardly tricks. The spectators are boorish, with that mob spirit that Lawrence hated. Before the wretched spectacle is half over Kate leaves, unescorted until the solicitous Viedma approaches her and conducts her to his waiting car. His courteous presence is in pointed contrast to that of the companions she has left, who are apparently still enjoying the bullfight.

A dialectic is thus established, in this first episode, between a brutish, death-loving Mexico, on the one hand, and that other Mexico of still potency which arrests her attention in Viedma: "He came through the people from the inner entrance, and cleared his way with a quiet, silent unobtrusiveness, yet with the peculiar heavy Indian momentum" (*PS,* p. 22).

There is a heaviness that is oppression, a deadly weight, a squalid underworld, the death wish within the culture; and there is a heaviness of gravity, a pull towards rooting, downwards to the center.[11] Viedma perceives Kate's ambivalence towards the heavy spirit of the country and clarifies her mingled sense of disgust and attraction.

"Mexico pulls you down, the people pull you down like a great weight! But it may be they pull you down as the earth's pull of gravitation does, that you can balance on your feet. Maybe they draw you down as the earth draws down the roots of a tree, so that it may be clinched deep in soil. Men are still part of the Tree of Life, and the roots go down to the centre of the earth. Loose leaves, and aeroplanes, blow away on the wind, in what they call freedom. But the Tree of Life has fixed, deep, gripping roots.

"It may be you need to be drawn down, down, till you send roots into the deep places again. Then you can send up the sap and the leaves back to the sky, later" (*PS,* pp. 85-86).

Mexicans, Viedma continues, have been uprooted, felled by Western culture, but the indigenous Indian sensibility is still at work to replant the forest, send roots down deep into the earth again. This is the purpose of the revived nationalist religion of Quetzalcoatl which Ramón is to inspire and Viedma to mobilize.

"A fresh start, in the first great direction, with the polarity downwards"[12]—this is by no means a new idea for Lawrence. His mythicizing imagination had early invested the dust-smeared dark miners walking home from the pit with attributes of chthonic beings: a magnetism of unseeing connection. From Walter Morel's visionless sensuality to the powerful sense of touch in "The Blind Man," to Lady Chatterley's insistence on the rootedness rather than the upward growing nature of flowers, to the passionate meditation on the dark underworld in "Bavarian Gentians," Lawrence persistently explored that dialectic between roots and leaves, origin and utterance, earth and air.

For Kate, as for Lawrence, European culture has become heady, abstracted, overburdened by mind, refusing to recognize that—in the words of

Norman O. Brown—"Knowledge is carnal knowledge, ... What is always speaking silently is the body."[13] Man short-circuits his sense of reality by referring experience directly to mental processes, thus losing the validation of the organism. He establishes authenticity instead through preconceived ideas, the leaves of the tree which he tries to keep from perishing, rather than trusting to the rootedness of the tree to produce new leaves in the due passage of time.

For Lawrence, true morality, as opposed to that of his time, draws from the roots; it is "only an instinctive adjustment which the soul makes in every circumstance, adjusting one thing to another livingly, delicately, sensitively."[14] The interchange between the self and the body of the world is a constantly changing dance.

But there needs an education of the self that is lost to us, who have overdeveloped the upper centers at the expense of the solar plexus, the wellspring of thought. "I wake to sleep," writes Theodore Roethke, "and take my waking slow."

> I feel my fate in what I cannot fear.
> I learn by going where I have to go.
>
> We think by feeling. What is there to know?
> I hear my being dance from ear to ear.
> I wake to sleep, and take my waking slow.

In Lawrence's words, "The supreme lesson of human consciousness is to learn how *not* to *know*. That is, how not to *interfere*."[15] The overdeveloped mental consciousness feels according to habitual notions about feeling, thinks by repetition of other thinkers' repetitions.

Of course Lawrence is too intelligent a thinker to deny the importance, the necessity, of thought; but it is the *order* of things that he is concerned to redirect.

> This does not mean that man should immediately cut off his head and try to develop a pair of eyes in his breasts. But it does mean this: that an idea is just the final concrete or registered result of living dynamic interchange and reactions: that no idea is ever perfectly expressed until its dynamic cause is finished; ... The idea, the actual idea, must rise ever fresh, ever displaced, like the leaves of a tree, from out of the quickness of the sap.[16]

By the misuse of the power of the will we force the leaves to remain on the tree; the old fine impulses of love, benevolence, sympathy, idealism—all these have lost their ground in a real connection of sympathetic attraction, person to person, have become petrified into dogma and hung on to desperately as a narcissistic means of satisfying what Roethke calls "the soul's authentic hunger." They are now mere mental possessions which the individual draws into himself in the greedy and compulsive exercise of the will.

So Carlota, in *The Plumed Serpent*, that most Christian lady, is caught in the toils of a willed charity that sucks her life and is fast destroying that of her sons. The impulse to kindness and sympathy is dead in her, but she clings the more desperately to charitable activities—like her male counterpart, Thomas Crich in *Women in Love*.

For Kate, the downthrust of Mexican life, as glimpsed in Cipriano, in Ramón, in the peons of the village, in the very vegetation and air of Mexico, while it is repulsive and oppressive, attracts her too with the intimation of release. Lawrence speaks of the "dangerous overbalance of the natural psyche." Clearly part of the task for the revived religion of Quetzalcoatl is to right this imbalance, as Kate is to learn, later, in a ritual dance, "to loosen the uplift of all her life, and let it pour slowly, darkly, with an ebbing gush, rhythmical in soft, rhythmic gushes from her feet into the dark body of the earth" (*PS*, p. 141).

I have described the initial episode of *The Plumed Serpent*, that of the bullfight, as setting up a dialectic for Kate of attraction and repulsion with regard to the heavy spirit of Mexico. As I said, the scene also provides an initial image of that atomistic devolution in relationships that is so jarring to Kate as she witnesses the pitiful spectacle and its effect on the spectators, Mexican and American: in contrast, she meets with the sympathetic courtesy of Viedma.

In the following episode, that in which she goes to visit Mrs. Norris, a similar ambivalent sense of Mexico is created. Kate is again struck by the squalid atmosphere of the place: the ugly and dilapidated buildings, peons loafing at the corner of the street half drunk on *pulque,* an air of persistent, almost willed, neglect. The conversation at Mrs. Norris's gathering turns inevitably on the curious death-drift of the culture, in the apparent enjoyment of exploitation and criminality. Mexico's ultimate goal seems to be "Viva la Muerte." Mrs. Norris herself views Mexico in the spirit of humorous resignation, and attends to her flourishing garden.[17] Kate admires her for her lonely, strong-willed individuality; she is a woman much like Kate herself in this respect. Yet for all her gracious and interesting hospitality, Mrs. Norris has a coercive effect on the group, so that the atmosphere becomes charged with irritability, with a sense of force. The other guests talk constantly, and abrasively. In particular, Mrs. Burlap, baby-faced and pallid, and her ill-tempered husband focus the disharmony that Kate feels in the group. A different sense of value comes over her at the end of the evening as she contemplates the slightly drunk Mexicans standing on the side of the road.

Stronger than her fear was a certain sympathy with these dark-faced silent men in their big straw hats and naive little cotton blouses. Anyhow they had blood in their veins: they were columns of dark blood.

Whereas the other bloodless, acidulous couple from the Middle-West, with their nasty whiteness... ! (*PS*, p. 50).

So Kate turns forty wondering why she has come to "this high plateau of death"—oppressive, cruel, destructive; but also harboring that other spirit, that "certain sensitive tenderness of the heavy blood," an elusive silent responsiveness to the steady beatings of the pulse of the earth. Perhaps, paradoxically, it is here in Mexico that she can "be alone with the unfolding of her own soul, in the delicate chiming silence that is in the midst of things" (*PS,* pp. 53, 54, 64).

The religious revival initiated by Ramón provides a focus for the quest toward that peace intimated to Kate in the unwilled gesture of the native Mexicans and in the forceful presences of Cipriano and Ramón. Quetzalcoatl, the bird of the air and the serpent of the earth, provides a symbol for that equipoise of being in which upper and lower centers are in balance and the self collects itself, not in vehemence or assertion but in a listening attunement to its world. So Lawrence believed; and so Kate, in the novel, begins to understand.

> To shut doors of iron against the mechanical world. But to let the sunwise world steal across to her, and add its motion to her, the motion of the stress of life, with the big sun and the stars like a tree holding out its leaves (*PS,* pp. 112-13).

She is weary of the clattering talk that attempts to obliterate time; tired of the accomplished self, complete in isolation; she seeks an alternative to the sapless ideal of benevolence which no longer draws nourishment from the roots of passionate faith. Instead she looks for the silence that will calm her assertive will, that may allow her to listen to herself, and to find a transcendence of possessive desire that makes way for the fuller erotic realization of what the Buddhist calls "suchness."

> If we would meet in the quick, we must give up the assembled self, the daily I, and putting off ourselves one after the other, meet unconscious in the Morning Star. Body, soul and spirit can be transfigured into the Morning Star (*PS,* p. 270).

For Quetzalcoatl—as Ramón tries to explain to Carlota, who is horrified at his sacrilege—is only an image expressive of a mode of being in the world.

> "Quetzalcoatl is just a living word, for these people, no more. All I want them to do is to find the beginnings of the way to their own manhood, their own womanhood" (*PS,* pp. 224-25).

The plumed serpent, the morning star, Pan, the Holy Spirit, the opening of the third eye, the dragon of the cosmos: all are icons of the soul's transfiguration, of its awakening from the sleep of solipsism.

So Kate is gradually initiated into the new religion through a series of deaths and awakenings; just as in the apocalypse of love in *The Rainbow* and

Women in Love, the characters develop through a series of birthings which necessarily involve the death of the old self—a phoenix-conflagration.

As she is being rowed up the lake to Orilla, Kate encounters a naked swimmer who demands tribute to Quetzalcoatl, the tutelary spirit of the lake. After a minute or two the demand fades, with the words "We will wait till the Morning Star rises." The boatman pulls away, and Kate, looking at the swimmer, sees "the peculiar gleaming far-awayness, suspended between the realities, which . . . [is] the central look in the native eyes" (*PS,* p. 98). The boatman too is arrested in the momentary beauty of illumination, an instant of stasis that transforms his face, causing Kate suddenly to address him: "You have the morning star in your eyes" (*PS,* p. 99). Kate realizes that a dramatic change has occurred in her, an opening to some mystery of such delicacy that she dreads the intrusion of her companion, Villiers. The moment passes; the vibrant quiet becomes again that silence of "vacuity, arrest, and cruelty" in the vicious chemical conflict that is the air of Mexico.

But the revelation comes to her again, unbidden. As the motor boat takes her down the lake to her new home in the village of Sayula, she becomes strongly aware of the presence of the two Mexican boatmen: she fears their cruelty, their incipient will to destruction. Then another sense takes over—a feeling of peace and trust in the greater mystery which transforms the petty intentions of individuals; and quietly she shares with the men the oranges and sandwiches that she has brought with her.

> As he peeled his orange and dropped the yellow peel on the water, she could see the stillness, the humility, and the pathos of grace in him; something very beautiful and truly male, and very hard to find in a civilized white man. It was not of the spirit. It was of the dark, strong, unbroken blood, the flowering of the soul (*PS,* p. 116).

As she lands in Sayula and leaves the boatmen, she feels grateful for the journey they have soundlessly shared. "Concrete, jarring exasperating reality had melted away, and a soft world of potency stood in its place, the velvety dark flu from the earth, the delicate yet supreme life-breath in the inner air" (*PS,* p. 117). The house she then decides to rent reflects such quiet, with its flowery inturned patio, cool stone, still water, and deep shade.

But again comes the revulsion, the ambivalent reality of Mexico, reflected in Juana, whose warmth and fiery generosity alternate with the malevolent mockery of indifference.

As Kate grows more aware of the importance to her of staying in Mexico, the possibility of Ramón's religious revival appears less strange, more congruent with her needs. She watches the men in the plaza listening to the drums of Quetzalcoatl and is overcome by the physical power of their presence, which repels and fascinates her.

Here and here alone, it seemed to her, life burned with a deep new fire. The rest of life, as she knew it, seemed wan, bleached and sterile. The pallid wanness and weariness of her world! and here, the dark, ruddy figures in the glare of a torch, like the centre of the everlasting fire, surely this was a new kindling of mankind! (*PS*, pp. 130-31).

Yet again she remains on the fringe. Reluctantly, inevitably, as the men begin to dance she is drawn into the orbit of their motion; she responds to the guttural song in the depths of her heart, not outwardly; and as women join the men in alternating wheels of movement, she begins at last to tread the dance step, lost to her own individuality, at one with the slow-wheeling motion and absorbed in the erotic pulse of the dance. Returning home later, she feels herself radically changed by the event, newly aware of "the strange secret of her greater womanhood," and before she sleeps she hears again the drum "like a pulse inside a stone beating" (*PS*, p. 141).

The next episode, the chapter called "Night in the House," calls into question the validity of the drum's call to the dance: is it not the expression of outworn savage modes of being, the old rhythms of murder and lust? But then belief asserts itself again as she ponders the matter:

We must go back to pick up old threads. We must take up the old, broken impulse that will connect us with the mystery of the cosmos again, now we are at the end of our own tether (*PS*, p. 147).

Always there is the seesaw of revelation and its repudiation. In *The Rainbow* and *Women in Love* the ebb of denial comes after the moment of seeing; but, as I have argued, the impulse of connection, the will to faith, retains its primacy. In *The Plumed Serpent* Lawrence is less sure of the implications of that new world that he begins to envision. For Ramón, the process of change within him is "a slow, blind imperative, urging him to cast his emotional and spiritual and mental self into the slow furnace, and smelt them into a new, whole being" (*PS*, p. 221). Carlota hangs on to the old self of her husband, but he persists in his self-transmutation, declaring himself "nauseated with humanity and the human will: even with my own will" (*PS*, p. 78). Kate realizes that he is at the end of a road she has not yet herself finished traveling. It seems as though here, as elsewhere in his characterization of Kate, Lawrence is writing of his own position; he senses a new call in the air, but is unsure of the particulars of its utterance, as they will work out in the specifics of action. There is, therefore, a continual repudiation of the apocalyptic event in Kate's consciousness.

It is only after the attack on Ramón at his hacienda in Jamiltepec that her conversion seems apparently complete, her initiation into the religion of Quetzalcoatl performed. After she has witnessed the slaying of Ramón's servants and his own near death, and has been instrumental in saving his life, it seems that a profound alteration has taken place in her, a death.

The common threads that bound her to humanity seemed to have snapped. The little human things didn't interest her any more. Her eyes seemed to have gone dark, and blind to individuals (*PS*, p. 327).

She lives as one who has perished, yet awaits her renewal; she knows that a frail light burns within her—the illumination that has been the light kindled within her by Ramón, who has extinguished the "world-activities" of her former life. Now is the twilight of waiting. It is then Cipriano comes to visit her and she experiences the abandonment of herself to his power—"the vast, unspoken twilight of the Pan world" (*PS*, p. 333).

It is a curious transfer of sexual allegiance. The erotic power that draws Kate to Ramón culminates in her presence as his rescuer in the attempted assassination, an event which, because of her role in it, has a strong erotic undercurrent; the attraction that, we understand, she feels for Ramón is resolved only when she submits at last to Cipriano. The meeting between Kate and Cipriano is an unconvincing event: overblown, indeed hectic in language, absurd in its distortion of the idea of Pan, which elsewhere Lawrence had finely controlled. Coming as it does after the attack on Ramón, the handling of the scene evidences what is to be the geological fault of the novel, which from here on causes a series of earthquakes that topple the novel's structure.

Kate is apparently more committed to the new life after the attack on Ramón. As Malintzi, she marries Cipriano; she participates in the opening of the church to the gods of Quetzalcoatl, and she shares the vengeance and the vigil of Huitzilopochtli. Yet she participates now in a different way, as a victim, trespassed; and this unease flares up.

"Let me get out of this, and back to simple human people. I loathe the very sound of Quetzalcoatl and Huitzilopochtli. I would die rather than be mixed up in it any more"(*PS*, p. 396).

She is shocked by the savage executions of Huitzilopochtli, fears and loathes the exertions of the will, the drive to power in Ramón and Cipriano; and especially the will of Cipriano, which seems to her to be negating her own sense of being: "she was but the stone of rest of his potency, his bed of sleep, the cave and lair of his male will" (*PS*, p. 415). Naturally enough, she resists such relationship, and we remember Ramón's own rejection of this kind of meeting as between "ravisher" and "ravished." Such meetings must be transmuted: "Oh, if we could only abide by our own souls, and meet in the abiding place" (*PS*, p. 291). In *Women in Love*, Lawrence had a much more poised sense of the commitment of Birkin and Ursula to each other. So Birkin is able to declare,

"I deliver *myself* over to the unknown, in coming to you, I am without reserves or defenses, stripped entirely, into the unknown. Only there needs the pledge between us, that we will both cast off everything, cast off ourselves even, and cease to be, so that which is perfectly ourselves can take place in us" (*WIL*, p. 138).

The events after the assassination attempt take on a fevered intensity. I have mentioned the overblown and obfuscated analysis of Kate's sense of Cipriano, her "demon lover." Lawrence's description of the marriage ceremony does little to relieve the overcharged atmosphere, with its mixture of coy sentimentality and assertive rhetoric.

> Kate went up to her room and found a big earthenware bath with steaming water, and big towels. Also, in a beautiful little bowl, oil, and a soft bit of white wool.
> She bathed her rain-wet body in the warm water, dried and anointed herself with the clear oil, that was clear as water. It was soft, and had a faint perfume, and was grateful to the skin. She rubbed all her body, even among her hair and under her feet, till she glowed softly (*PS,* p. 353).

However, the inward grace that is ritualized—the idea of the abiding place—is finely conceived and powerfully effected elsewhere in Lawrence: in, for example, the meeting of Birkin and Ursula, the night of gathering sheaves undertaken by Will and Anna, the coming together of Tom and Lydia. In *The Plumed Serpent* the marriage ritual organizes an inward exaltation that has not been actualized in the relationship between Cipriano and Kate.

As the new religious practices continue, relationships between the participants become for the reader more distorted, almost hallucinatory, as in the case of the opening of the church, in which the men of Huitzilopochtli dance round a fire, naked but for a breech-cloth and bedecked with scarlet feathers. We are to understand that from Ramón and Cipriano a new world is unfolding, "unrolling, as softly and subtly as twilight falling and removing the clutter of day" (*PS,* p. 384). The reader is unconvinced: for evidence of such delicate awakening we have the crude brutality of Huitzilopochtli's Night, Cipriano's bloodthirsty militarism, and the machismo of his relationship with Kate, as well as the false mysticism of Ramón's transference to Cipriano of Quetzalcoatl's power. We understand Teresa through what she says about her love for Ramón, but no evidence of it comes through in the action; she remains a willed figure, necessary to the idea of the plot.

Altogether, it is clear that Lawrence is as unconvinced as Kate. He understands what has gone wrong with modern life, but is unable to effect the specifics of a program of renewal. Such a program of renewal was to be required again, in the unfinished narrative "The Flying Fish," written just after *The Plumed Serpent.* Lawrence told the Brewsters that the last part would deal with regenerate man—"a real life in the garden of Eden." But when they asked him how it would be, he was unable to answer.[18]

What goes wrong in *The Plumed Serpent?* In view of Lawrence's insistence on the necessity of a shift to the lower plexuses, it is interesting that what elicits our sense of the inauthenticity of the later scenes of the novel is their abstract, *voulu* quality—their lack of incarnation.

To try to understand this more clearly I should like to discuss an unfinished book which Lawrence had written ten years before *The Plumed Serpent:* "Study of Thomas Hardy"; for in this argument we may catch a clue as to Lawrence's difficulties in the development of his vision, and particularly as it is found in this problematic novel.

"Study of Thomas Hardy" is a compendious analysis of Hardy's novels, incorporating what Lawrence called "a kind of story of my heart or a *Confessio Fidei.*" In the introductory sections Lawrence declares that, in a time of the solemn declarations of patriotism of a nation preparing for war, work and politics are mere evasions of living; "your business is to produce your own real life no matter what the nations do."[19] The task is to achieve in one's own kind an intrinsic flowering, "the magical spurt of being which is a hare all-explosive with fulness of self, in the moonlight" ("Study," p. 403). This self draws from the transhuman power that Lawrence refers to so frequently at this time, cautiously and indirectly; below the human emotions and needs "are the tremendous unknown forces of life, coming unseen and unperceived as out of the desert to the Egyptians, and driving us, forcing us, destroying us if we do not submit to be swept away."[20] Hardy's genius, as Lawrence finds it, is that he draws upon this source as the central insight of the novels.

> The Heath persists. Its body is strong and fecund, it will bear many more crops beside this. Here is the sombre, latent power that will go on producing, no matter what happens to the product. Here is the deep, black source from whence all these little contents of lives are drawn ("Study," p. 415).

Hardy shares with the great masters such as Shakespeare, Sophocles, and Tolstoy

> this setting behind the small action of his protagonists the terrific action of unfathomed nature; setting a smaller system of morality, the one grasped and formulated by the human consciousness within the vast, uncomprehended and incomprehensible morality of nature or of life itself, surpassing human consciousness ("Study," p. 419).

But Hardy's insight fails in his conscious denying of the primacy of this force, so that

> the lesser, human morality, the mechanical system is actively transgressed, and holds, and punishes the protagonist, whilst the greater morality is only passively, negatively transgressed, it is represented merely as being present in background, in scenery, not taking any active part, having no direct connection with the protagonist ("Study," p. 420).

Lawrence finds in Hardy a visionary force that calls into question the inviolability of the social context to which the characters, and the author, finally submit. The power of the earth transmits to men a sense of vitality which has its own directives, directives more imperative than the temporary ethical orderings of a culture.

In the course of the same essay, Lawrence develops the idea of creative activity of any kind as being engendered by the polarized energies of male and female, "as if life were a double cycle, of men and women, facing opposite ways, traveling opposite ways, revolving upon each other" ("Study," p. 449). Elaborating on the polarities, he considers the female force as carrying the qualities of immutability, permanence, eternality—its analogue, drawn by reference to the Christian history, being (strangely) the First Person to the Trinity, the Father, the Law. Complementing the female movement, male force is the energy of motion, word, spirit, the Second Person of the Trinity, Christ, Love. In the Father we are one flesh, in Christ we are one with him in spirit.

These complementary dualities are not, of course, peculiar to Lawrence's vision of the energies of the cosmos. The Chinese "Book of Changes," the *I Ching,* for example, is based on a similar polarity of Yin and Yang. The first hexagram—Ch'ien: the Creative, Heaven—draws from the male energy, the "primal power, which is light-giving, active, strong, and of the spirit.... Its energy is represented as unrestricted by any fixed conditions in space and is therefore conceived of as motion." Its opposite—K'un: the Receptive, Earth— the second hexagram, "represents the dark, yielding, receptive primal power of yin. The attribute of the hexagram is devotion; its image is the earth." The Receptive does not normally combat the Creative, but complements it. It represents "nature in contrast to spirit, earth in contrast to heaven, space as against time, the female-maternal as against the male-paternal.... Indeed, even in the individual this duality appears in the coexistence of the spiritual world and the world of the senses."[21]

Lawrence develops the idea that all utterance—as all living—suffers from the imperfect complementarity of the dualities; but that the moment of artistic stasis, or the experienced full moment, is the moment of their near-equal union: Ramón's Morning Star.

Artistic form is a revelation of the two principles of Love and the Law in a state of conflict and yet reconciled: pure motion and struggling against and yet reconciled with the Spirit: active force meeting and overcoming and yet not overcoming inertia ("Study," p. 477).

In all but the greatest works of art there is constant antinomy between Law and Love, Father and Son, Flesh and Spirit. The ultimate reconcilement between Nature and Knowledge would be by way of the third person of the Trinity—the Holy Spirit—which is the completion of opposites, the hidden lure of artistic endeavor, the quick spark of revelation, the elusive insight whose form is constantly in flux.

According to Lawrence's argument, Hardy is a writer who derives his power from attention to the female force, although consciously he denies its power in his work. "His feeling, his instinct, his sensuous understanding is, however, apart from his metaphysic, very great and deep, . . . Always he must start from the earth" ("Study," p. 480). The theory of knowledge and the metaphysic in Hardy are much less profound than the whole vision.

Lawrence finds this division crucial to the novelist's struggle towards truth of utterance.

> It is the novelists and dramatists who have the hardest task in reconciling their metaphysic, their theory of being and knowing, with the living sense of being. Because a novel is a microcosm, and because man in viewing the universe must view it in the light of a theory, therefore every novel must have the background or the structural skeleton of some theory of being, some metaphysic. But the metaphysic must always subserve the artistic purpose beyond the artist's conscious aim. Otherwise the novel becomes a treatise ("Study," p. 479).

So it is, also, with morality: "every work of art adheres to some system of morality. But if it be really a work of art, it must contain the essential criticism on the morality to which it adheres" ("Study," p. 476). Hardy, lacking such ruthlessness, falls short of the greatest utterance.

Lawrence's interest in and perceptiveness concerning Hardy's failure point up an antimony in his own work between Law and Love, between what he knew and what he knew he knew. Lawrence, like Hardy, has a powerful sensuous understanding, a faculty of image-making in which equivalences present themselves as "a steady storm of correspondences." At the same time, he strives to understand the meaning of such awareness:

> The woman grows downwards, like a root, towards the center and the darkness and the origin. The man grows upwards, like the stalk, towards discovery and light and utterance ("Study," p. 514).

In the most successful scenes in Lawrence's work—as, for example, throughout *Women in Love*—there is a continued dialectic of enactment and analysis.

Lawrence is always drawn by an urgent sense of the need to discover new values, more authentic modes of relationship, new ways in which to explore emerging consciousness. *"What next?"* he writes, "That's what interests me. 'What now?' is no fun any more."[22] In *The Rainbow* and *Women in Love* he draws on his sensuous vision of natural correspondences to create an image of self-confrontation between persons. He then finds himself called upon to carry that intimation of new grounds of relationship beyond the individual's participation in the reciprocal apocalypse of love. In 1920, at the age of thirty-five, Lawrence wrote:

> When a man approaches the beginning of maturity and the fulfillment of his individual self, about the age of thirty-five, then is not his time to come to rest. On the contrary. Deeply fulfilled through marriage, and at one with his own soul, he must now undertake the

responsibility for the next step into the future. He must now give himself perfectly to some further purpose, some passionate purposive activity.[23]

The phase of generativity—to use Erikson's characterization of such a period—presents Lawrence with a dilemma: on the one hand, as an irrepressible moralist, he yearns to articulate a program for the organized dissemination of his powerfully held beliefs. Yet at the same time, as a novelist, he must back away from such promptings. "The degree to which the system of morality, or the metaphysic, of any work of art is submitted to criticism within the work of art makes the lasting value and satisfaction of that work"("Study," p. 476).

A deepening disillusionment with the encroaching industrialism and materialism of his society, clarified by persistent opposition to the war and by humiliating experiences as a civilian victim of the military; a constantly disappointed dream of Utopian brotherhood through the founding of a loving community; the frustrations of marriage, which in the quotidian often seemed unsubmissive to his vision of Eden—it was difficulties such as these that sent Lawrence on the restless journeying that was the physical counterpart to his spiritual search to discover and write about "what the heart really wants for the next future."

However, during the years of his journeying, a truly adequate strategy for "breaking a way into the future" eludes him. The sensuous understanding of apocalypse, the revelation of connection, which was the power center of the earlier novels, devolves often into abstraction in *Aaron's Rod, Kangaroo,* and *The Plumed Serpent.* To use the terms that he had developed in the Hardy study, the principle of the second person of the Trinity, the Son, in the sense of motility and abstraction, dominates the principle of the Father—the apprehended but unexplained incarnation of the living cosmos. Lawrence had grasped, in *The Rainbow* and *Women in Love,* a sense of creatures living their own strange lives, ineluctably in connection with one another; but he finds himself unable now to translate personal revelation into political renewal, with an authenticity answerable to the theme of transfiguration.

Regeneration in *The Plumed Serpent* is found not in the liturgy and ritual events of the new religion, nor in the hierogamy of Kate and Cipriano; nor is it discovered through the magnetic presence of Ramón, or the military panache of Cipriano. Rather, just as in Hardy's works the ground, that from which the argument derives its power, is found in the interstices of the argument, so to speak. In *The Plumed Serpent,* that sense of being in touch with the life of the cosmos, which it is the function both of the new religion for the people and of Kate's personal initiation to discover, is found largely in the interstices of the plot. Pan will not be hunted, but lurks in the underbrush, choosing his own moments of apparition.

The narrative works, it seems, in those places in which the symbol reaches into ancient connections, in which events are related to other events not by causality but by analogy and correspondence; or in those scenes in which the writer's sense of life transmutes ordinary reality into an event of importance— the gift demonstrated so consistently in *Sons and Lovers,* as in *The Rainbow* and *Women in Love.* The symbolic scene, and the transmutation of the ordinary into the important, carries the validation for the reader of Lawrence's belief in the living cosmos. Much of the time this validation is found in *The Plumed Serpent* not at crucial points in the plot, but in what might be called the "negative spaces" of the narrative.

In painting, the ground around the figures is an important, though often unnoticed element in the composition, controlling as it does both the tonal quality of the figures themselves in relation to the ground, and the relation of the figures one to another. Though subdominant in the total composition, these "negative spaces," as they are often called, must be sufficiently determined to be perceived in their own right.[24] In *The Plumed Serpent,* the so-called "background," including minor plot elements, is given sufficient figure quality so that these negative spaces stand in clear relation to the major events of the plot itself; they are, as in the case of a painting, an important element in our reception of the whole novel.

During the marriage between Kate and Cipriano, Ramón invokes the spirit of the morning star in which the two find the basis of their relationship. There is a cloying prissiness to the event, as well as a forced sense of ritual, with its grab bag of contrived symbols. However, an earlier, much smaller event carries the inward and spiritual grace that Lawrence lacked in the formal ritual. For a moment the Morning Star of perfect sympathy, of pure trust, hangs between Kate and her boatman as she rows up the lake to Orilla.

> He watched Kate's face with that gleaming, intense semi-abstraction, a gleam that hung unwavering in his black eyes, and which suddenly reminded Kate of the morning star, or the evening star, hanging perfect between night and the sun.
> "You have the morning star in your eyes," she said to the man.
> He flashed her a smile of extraordinary beauty.
> "The Señorita understands," he said.
> His face changed again to a dark-brown mask, like semitransparent stone, and he rowed with all his might (*PS,* p. 99).

The sense of wonder is found in small events. Mrs. Norris's garden is vividly rendered as a tropical underworld, glowing with visionary intensity.

> It was like being at the bottom of some dusky, flowering garden down in Hades. Hibiscus hung scarlet from the bushes, putting out yellow bristling tongues. Some roses were scattering scentless petals on the twilight, and lonely-looking carnations hung on weak stalks. From a huge dense bush the mysterious white bells of the datura were suspended,

large and silent, like the very ghosts of sound. And the datura scent was moving thick and noiseless from the tree, into the little alleys (*PS*, p. 48).

Lawrence's description of the lake creates an image of lustration more effectively than does the narrative of Ramón's ritual before the coming of the rain; there is in the description of early morning on the water a delicacy, fluidity, and sweetness that is the physical counterpart of those qualities Ramón invokes in the new religion.

> Morning was still young on the pale buff river, between the silent earthen banks. There was a blue dimness in the lower air, and black water-fowl ran swiftly, unconcernedly back and forth from the river's edge, on the dry, baked banks that were treeless now, and wider. They had entered a wide river, from the narrow one. The blueness and the moistness of the dissolved night seemed to linger under the scattered pepper-trees of the far shore (*PS*, p. 96).

One could multiply examples of the intensity of seeing in the novel. There are the street vendors in the plaza arranging their wares, "lifting with small sensitive brown hands the little toys they had so carefully made and painted" (*PS*, p. 54). Or the man selling oranges, "wiping them with a cloth so carefully, almost tenderly, and piling them in bright tiny pyramids, all neat and exquisite" (*PS*, p. 54). The unbelievable staleness of Mexico is an almost physically airless presence to us as we read about the weary train ride to Ixtlahuacan. Then there is the realized eroticism of the writer's description of the peons in the plaza:

> Those men who sat there in their dark, physical tenderness, so still and soft, they looked at the same time frightening. Something dark, heavy, and reptilian in their silence and their softness. Their very naked torsos were clothed with a subtle shadow, a certain secret obscurity (*PS*, p. 130).

Even the account of Kate's servants' lives is done with such attentiveness that the very quick of the motion of life seems grasped as it passes.

> No, it was no sinecure, being a Niña. At dawn began the scrape-scrape of the twig broom outside. Kate stayed on in bed, doors fastened but shutters open. Flutter outside! Somebody wanted to sell two eggs. Where is the Niña? She is sleeping! The visitor does not go. Continual flutter outside.
>
> The *aguador!* Ah, the water for the Niña's bath! She is sleeping, she is sleeping. "No!" called Kate, slipping into a dressing-gown and unbolting the door. In come the children with the bath tub, in comes the *aguador* with the two square kerosene cans full of hot water. Twelve centavos! Twelve centavos for the *aguador! No hay!* We haven't got twelve centavos. Later! Later! Away trots the *aguador,* pole over his shoulder (PS, p. 150).[25]

Symbols, for Lawrence,

> stand for units of human *feeling,* human experience. A complex of emotional experience is a symbol. And the power of the symbol is to arouse the deep emotional self, and the dynamic

self, beyond comprehension. Many ages of accumulated experience still throb within a symbol.[28]

Many of the most vividly realized moments in *The Plumed Serpent* occur in the negative spaces of the action. However, there are one or two episodes that seem to be more central to the novel's structure and do exhibit real symbolic power, a power deriving from "many ages of accumulated experience," in contrast to the contrived symbolic arrangements of the rituals of Quetzalcoatl.

One such symbol is the lake, whose milky water soothes Kate's irritation at the abrasive temper of Mexico and helps to dissolve her feeling of loathing towards the country, so that she is ready to understand the swimmer's gesture of faith and, on a later journey, to establish a sense of trust in her Mexican boatmen. I have discussed the appearance of the swimmer of Quetzalcoatl as an example of Lawrence's use of negative space—as a spontaneous illumination with the reality, but none of the panoply, of the invocation to the Morning Star in Ramón's marriage ceremony. However, as the novel progresses, the lake becomes an image of more pervasive importance: it assumes more dominant figure quality (just as in the well-known figure of two faces looking at each other in profile, the ground may, at another looking, become the figure of the design, in the form of a vase, or urn). Thus the goal, the new *axis mundi*, to which Kate journeys repeatedly and with increasing urgency, is the hacienda of Ramón, which is reached by boat; the lake symbolizes, then, Kate's inner journey towards acceptance of the sense of life held by Ramón and Cipriano. The epiphanies which occur on the lake—the boatman's gesture of illumination as he contemplates the swimmer's message, the communion of grace which Kate feels she has shared with the boatman—these, as manifestations of the spirit of the lake, are agents of Kate's conversion, and the answer to her cry: *"Give me the mystery and let the world live again for me!... And deliver me from man's automatism"* (*PS*, p. 113).[27]

The other event that has special symbolic force is the ritual dance in which Kate participates—an important revelation to her of a reality beyond the boundaries of the isolated self. It is also the only scene in the novel in which the physical intensity of the episode as transpersonal event matches the power of Lawrence's finest writing in *The Rainbow* and *Women in Love*. In the course of the account the reader is drawn into the pulsing rhythms of the event through the strength and repetitive intensity of the writing:

> The song seemed to take new wild flights, after it had sunk and rustled to a last ebb. It was like waves that rise out of the invisible, and rear up into form and a flying, disappearing whiteness and a rustle of extinction. And the dancers, after dancing in a circle in a slow, deep absorption, each man changeless in his own place, treading the same dust with the soft, churning of bare feet, slowly, slowly began to revolve, till the circle was slowly revolving around the fire, with always the same soft, down-sinking, churning tread (*PS*, p. 137).

The repetitive ebb and flow of the prose enacts the motion of the dance—the two circles of men and women wheeling in opposite directions darkly moving by touch and weight. The visual images are few; Lawrence proceeds in mimesis of the heavy tactile pull of the rhythm. As we read we understand the symbol of the dance through a somatic response to the movement of the prose.

In the preceding chapter I mentioned that Ursula, in *Women in Love,* was invested by Lawrence with some of the mythic attributes of the Woman Clothed with the Sun. Lawrence considered the presence of the Magna Mater in the book of Revelation one of its more interesting features. A religion of power needs a queen, he asserts, a bountiful cosmic mother, no matter how inimical this conception may be to religions of renunciation such as the Christianity of the writer of Revelation.[28]

It is therefore consistent that in Lawrence's pantheon a goddess would unite with the avatar of the gods in the *hieros gamos.* Kate, as she is seen through Cipriano's eyes, has some of the attributes of the Magna Mater. When he and she first meet, Cipriano is overwhelmed by the pathos of her sorrow as she remembers her first life.

> The wonder, the mystery, the magic that used to flood over him as a boy and a youth, when he kneeled before the babyish figure of the Santa Maria de la Soledad, flooded him again. He was in the presence of the goddess (*PS,* p. 76).

Again, at a later meeting he is entranced by the Madonna-like beauty of her repose. "She was the mystery, and he the adorer, under the semi-ecstatic spell of the mystery" (*PS,* p. 87). It is interesting that in both these instances Cipriano likens Kate to the image of Mary; the comparison is much less profound than is Birkin's understanding of the life-giving aspect of Ursula, who is seen by him as suffused with light, glowing with a golden warmth, enkindled in fire. The images surrounding Ursula draw from the imaginative springs that call into being images of the eternal renewal of nature, the biblical figure of the Woman Clothed with the Sun being but one manifestation of this archetypal impulse. However, in *The Plumed Serpent* Lawrence is unable to call forth the image in its depth: Kate is described as having some of the attributes of Mary; she wears the green flowered robe of the goddess as Malintzi, and is supposedly recreated to pristine virginity by the holy marriage with Huitzilopochtli. But this marriage contains little of the real tenderness and flowerlike delicacy created in the image of Ursula. The new awakening is a fact in *Women in Love,* an assertion in *The Plumed Serpent.* Beside the renewal of Ursula and Birkin in love, the holy marriage between Malintzi and Huitzilopochtli seems like a puppet show.

The writer's design was to create Kate as possessing some of the attributes and functions of the Magna Mater as the Woman Clothed with the Sun. In like manner Lawrence's portrayal of Ramón calls to mind the dying god Tammuz of Babylonian mythology (who later becomes the Greek Adonis). In Ramón's death and revival, events that form a central episode in the novel, Lawrence clearly draws on the power of the symbol of the god of perennial return. In this aspect Kate, who saves his life and who finds herself after the attack in a period of deathlike waiting, is the goddess Ishtar, the lover of Tammuz, who journeys to the underworld in quest of her dead consort, reclaiming him at last from the chthonic Allatar. During this time the upper earth mourns, and all creativity is suspended, until Ishtar returns with her lover.

> She felt that afternoon of bloodshed had blown all their souls into the twilight of death, for the time. But they would come back. They would come back. Nothing to do but to submit and wait. Wait, with a soul almost dead, and hands and heart of uttermost inert heaviness, indifference (*PS*, p. 328).

There is also, perhaps, some sense in which the opposition of Kate and Teresa represents the light and chthonic deities Ishtar and Allatar each desiring to possess Tammuz—or the conflict between Aphrodite and Persephone for the beautiful Adonis.

Lawrence believed that the book of Revelation, in its vengeful destruction of the power of the world, indicates the suppression of a natural yearning in man for splendor and mastery. "Every great king makes every man a little lord in his own tiny sphere, fills the imagination with lordship and splendour, satisfies the soul."[29] The powerful leader is an inspiration and model. Yet, he believes, within the book of Revelation can be found an incarnation of the spirit of power in the splendid Cosmocrator, fiery with the sun's strength. Suddenly, says Lawrence, "we see some of the old pagan splendour, that delighted in the might and the magnificence of the cosmos, and man who was as a star in the cosmos."[30] This is one of the images that Lawrence spoke of, in his related essay on the Apocalypse, as releasing the imagination to contemplate with awe the life of the universe. Ramón in his splendid presence evokes the god-like ruler, both in his power over his disciples and his transaction with death, his return from the underworld as "this pale, distant man, with a curious gleam, like a messenger from the beyond, in his soul" (*PS*, p. 338).

After writing *The Plumed Serpent*, Lawrence repudiated the image of a powerful leader who commands disciples by a natural aristocracy of spirit. *The Man Who Died* is Lawrence's retraction of the concept—his palinode—though, as *Apocalypse* testifies, the image of the glorious leader who is the human counterpart of the divine cosmocrator remains always alluring.

In *The Plumed Serpent*, as throughout his fiction, Lawrence attempts to incarnate the presences sensed beyond, or rather within, his physical world. In *The Rainbow*, when Tom is alone with his lambing ewes at night in the pasture, he looks out at the flashing stars with the certainty that "he did not belong to himself" (*Rainbow*, p. 35). So Ramón invokes the presence of Pan, the indwelling spirit of strange, other, mystery in the world. Lawrence tries to recreate the presences of the Aztec gods as a means of expressing his sense of immanent hierophany—every marriage partaking of the hierogamy, every psychic death and rebirth manifesting the gods' death and renewal.

> There are no gods, and you can please yourself
> have a game of tennis, go out in the car, do some
>   shopping, sit and talk, talk, talk
> with a cigarette browning your fingers.
>
> There are no gods, and you can please yourself—
> go and please yourself—
>
> But leave me alone, leave me alone, to myself!
> and then in the room, whose is the presence
> that makes the air so still and lovely to me?
>
> Who is it that softly touches the sides of my breast
> and touches me over the heart
> so that my heart beats soothed, soothed, soothed
>   and at peace?
>
>   . . . .
>
> Who is it that clasps and kneads my naked feet,
>   till they unfold,
> till all is well, till all is utterly well? the
>   lotus-lilies of the feet!
>
> I tell you, it is no woman, it is no man, for I
>   am alone.
> And I fall asleep with the gods, the gods
> that are not, or that are
> according to the soul's desire,
> like a pool into which we plunge, or do not plunge.[31]

But like Ramón, Lawrence as a writer "yearns for the sensual fulfillment of his soul." The organization of a religious revival as a means of opening the eyes of a society, through destruction of their outworn images and replacement by the program of renewal—this is, he realizes, a discarnate enterprise.

> I refuse to name the gods, because they have no name.
> I refuse to describe the gods, because they have
>   no form nor shape nor substance.
>
> Ah, but the simple ask for images!
> Then for a time at least, they must do without.—

But all the time I see the gods:
the man who is mowing the tall white corn,
suddenly, it curves, as it yields, the white wheat
and sinks down with the swift rustle, and a strange,
    falling flatness,
ah! the gods, the swaying body of god!
ah the fallen stillness of god, autumnus, and
    it is only July
the pale-gold flesh of Priapus dropping asleep.[32]

Lawrence seeks a reconcilement of Love and Law in the Holy Spirit. "When the two are acting together, then Life is produced, then Life, or Utterance, Something, is *created*. And nothing is or can be created save by combined efforts of the two principles, Law and Love" ("Study," p. 513). He strives to balance the complementary principles—the spirit of mobility, of knowledge having taken precedence in *The Plumed Serpent*. He invokes the Holy Spirit, "to give each party, Apollo and the Furies, Love and the Law, his due, and so to seek the Reconciler" ("Study," p. 514). This means for Lawrence, not a return to the world of *The Rainbow* or *Sons and Lovers*, for his knowledge of the social implications of such vision has gone too far. He has, like Wordsworth in a similar development of sensibility, understood himself to have assumed the responsibility of the prophet, who must continually call to an unhearing people for amendment of their ways.

In *The Plumed Serpent*, as in *Aaron's Rod* and *Kangaroo*, Lawrence moves closer than in earlier works to the apocalyptist's view of the hour for change as having passed, of catastrophe as being inevitable; though he always maintains a considerable degree of the prophet's belief in the individual's freedom to avert disaster by contrition and moral amendment. After *The Plumed Serpent* he is less interested in the apocalyptist's revelation and analysis of the inevitable cataclysm overtaking society. He is more concerned for the destiny of those who choose to change, more sympathetic to the prophet's trust in man as capable of self-transformation in the time of decision. Lawrence shares Blake's belief in the Last Judgment as an immanent reality within the individual, the judgment that passes upon such an individual when he "Rejects Error and Embraces Truth." Unlike Blake, however, he has the apocalyptist's and Old Testament prophet's sense of the historical hour as a time demanding inner change if destruction is to be averted; and it is the alternatives rather than the cataclysm that he is concerned to explore.[33]

Lawrence, in his search for the Holy Spirit as Reconciler, turns from political programs and the fate of society—the world of *Aaron's Rod, Kangaroo,* and *The Plumed Serpent*—to concern for the apocalypse within the individual as the seed crystal of societal change. "We must rise," says Norman O. Brown, "from history to mystery." And "to rise from history to mystery is to experience the resurrection of the body here now, as an eternal reality; to experience the *parousia,* the presence in the present, which is the spirit."[34]

> People were bathing and posturing themselves on
>   the beach
> and all was dreary, great robot limbs, robot breasts
> robot voices, robot even the gay umbrellas.
>
> But a woman, shy and alone, was washing herself
>   under a tap
> and the glimmer of the presence of the gods was
>   like lilies,
> and like water-lilies.[35]

5

Lady Chatterley's Lover: The Reality of Peace

In the second version of the novel finally published as *Lady Chatterley's Lover*—the version entitled *John Thomas and Lady Jane*—Connie one afternoon comes unexpectedly upon Parkin, the gamekeeper, washing himself behind his cottage. She is arrested by the naked beauty of the man, as he ducks his head into the soapy water, his velveteen breeches hanging low over his hips. Her reaction to such an ordinary sight both confuses and awes her.

> A great soothing came over her heart, along with the feeling of worship. The sudden sense of pure beauty, beauty that was active and alive, had put worship in her heart again. Not that she worshipped the man, nor his body. But worship had come into her, because she had seen a pure loveliness, that was alive, and that had touched the quick in her. It was as if she had touched God, and been restored to life.[1]

As Lawrence, in the poem quoted at the end of the previous chapter, found in the aspect of a certain woman washing herself under the tap the "glimmer of the gods," so Connie discovers in this mundane epiphany "the presence in the present, which is the spirit."[2]

Such a vision of "dust succinct with spirit" (to use John Gardner's words) is the subject of Lawrence's final major novel, *Lady Chatterley's Lover*, the narrative of which describes the coming of the Spirit to Connie and the gamekeeper, now called Mellors. "We fucked a flame into being," writes Mellors in a letter, at the end of the novel. And, "it's my Pentecost, the forked flame between me and you."[3] The forked flame, the spirit within and between Connie and Mellors, is another manifestation of the wayward power which Lawrence describes elsewhere as the visitation of Pan, the fluid movement of the coiling dragon of the universe, the dance of the dolphins, the lambent flame "wreathing through the cosmos for ever."[4]

I have presented the vision of Parkin-Mellors as Lawrence expresses it in his second writing of the novel that was to be *Lady Chatterley's Lover*. As he revised further, he came to understand his subject more clearly.

So she went round the side of the house. At the back of the cottage the land rose steeply, so the backyard was sunken, and enclosed by a low stone wall. She turned the corner of the house and stopped. In the little yard two paces beyond her, the man was washing himself, utterly unaware. He was naked to the hips, his velveteen breeches slipping down over his slender loins. And his white slim back was curved over a big bowl of soapy water, in which he ducked his head, shaking his head with a queer, quick little motion, lifting his slender white arms, and pressing the soapy water from his ears, quick, subtle as a weasel playing with water, and utterly alone (*LCL,* p. 75).

In the published novel Lawrence dwells longer on the actual sight of the man, his appearance and manner. Analysis of the event is reduced, and the revelation of the Divine, which had been the focus of the second version (also of "The First Lady Chatterley") gives place to an emphasis more resolutely incarnate: "Not the stuff of beauty, not even the body of beauty, but a lambency, the warm, white flame of a single life, revealing itself in contours that one might touch: a body!" (*LCL,* p. 76). The power of the experience for Connie draws not from beauty or divinity, except as these are embodied in that single event, the "ineluctable modality" of the actual presence of that man in that place: the individual revealed in the clarity of his "suchness."

If one comes to *Lady Chatterley's Lover* after reading *Aaron's Rod, Kangaroo,* or *The Plumed Serpent,* one is struck by a new quality in the writing: the tone is more contemplative, more chastened than formerly. One is puzzled, too, by the nature of the plot's development: it appears that such development is through intensification of an original experience of importance, both for the reader and the protagonists. That is, the plot does not so much unfold, as repeat and clarify a revelation offered early in the narrative. This lends a certain sense of peace to the narrative, the relaxation of onward striving; it is a motion markedly different from the intense and powerful spiralling movement of continual eschatological choice in *Women in Love;* or the restless oscillation of development in *The Plumed Serpent,* brought about in the dialectic of Kate's alternating skepticism and faith.

If the structure of *Women in Love* is like that of the double helix and that of *The Plumed Serpent* has an oscillatory movement, then the figure that *Lady Chatterley's Lover* puts one in mind of is that of a mandala.

It has been remarked that the ambiance of the novel possesses a circular configuration—the gamekeeper's hut being encircled by the wood, which is itself surrounded by the denatured landscape of mines, factories, and industrial towns. Moreover, the circle was one of Lawrence's most often employed images, meeting for him an inner sense of configuration.

Strange that we should think in straight lines, when there are none, and talk of straight courses, when every course, sooner or later, is seen to be making the sweep round, swooping upon the centre.... If I have a way to go, it will be round the swoop of a bend impinging centripetal towards the centre. The straight course is hacked out in wounds, against the will of the world.[5]

In an essay on Verga, and in *Apocalypse,* he writes of the emotional mind as essentially performing a circular, or perhaps—more accurately—a spiral motion. He was impressed, too, by the round dances of the New Mexico Indians; and L.D. Clark suggests that the circle is the central symbol and prevalent movement of *The Plumed Serpent* in Lawrence's imagination of a "roundward" universe.[6]

However, the mandala is a circle with a particular function: it is revelatory and conducive to contemplation. Mircea Eliade describes the use of the mandala in Tantric Hinduism as equivalent, for the disciple, to an act of initiation, issuing in a revelation of the universe as theophany. The mandala, he adds, defends the disciple against any destructive force, while at the same time helping him find his own center through contemplation.[7] Like any work of art *Lady Chatterley's Lover* is a special "protected ground"; but it also has both the revelatory and the contemplative aspects of the figure described by Eliade. It enables the reader to discover and dwell in a central event of clarified vision. The theophany is not new for Lawrence; but that quieter burning—"self-luminous, gentle, yet exalted," as Calvin Bedient describes it—this is new to Lawrence's fiction.

In the middle novels—*Aaron's Rod, The Plumed Serpent, Kangaroo*—as well as in essays such as *Fantasia of the Unconcious,* Lawrence was absorbed in a struggle to explain and disseminate his beliefs, with a prophetic passion for individual renovation. In the previous chapter I discussed the way in which Lawrence loses, at least partially, a necessary dialectic between insight and analysis in those works. The sensuous understanding of apocalypse as the revelation of connection between creatures of the phenomenal world—the power center of the earlier novels—becomes abstracted as Lawrence endeavors to create structures for renovation which would be based on a non-rational understanding of relatedness. He writes bitterly to Dr. Trigant Burrow, in June 1925, that people

lose the faculty for real experience, and go on decomposing their test-tubes full of social images. One fights and fights for that living something that stirs way down in the blood, and *creates* consciousness. But the world won't have it.[8]

As he struggles for more general acceptance of his beliefs, however, he seems to lose a receptivity necessary for their continuance. "One can fight for life," he has the narrator say in *John Thomas and Lady Jane,*

fight against the grey unliving armies, the armies of greedy ones and bossy ones, and the myriad host of the clutching and the self-important. Fight one does and must, against the enemies of life. But when you come to life itself, you must come as the flower does, naked and defenceless and infinitely in touch (*John Thomas*, p. 108).

Like Wordsworth, the substance of whose vision was likewise essentially inexpressible "breathings for incommunicable powers," Lawrence finds that the necessary imposition of conscious categorizing and analysis obscures his vision. There is a certain self-disgust in Lawrence's portrayal of Clifford as the writer who reduces his experience by verbalizing it. At the same time, Lawrence reverences the writer as having gifts that bring into being a powerful agent of sympathy and far-reaching change; the novel is "the one bright book of life," revelatory and healing. In this he is again like Wordsworth, who saw himself as continuing the prophetic line of Sidney, Spenser, and Milton, bringing into consciousness passional truths hitherto unperceived.

Behind Lawrence's dislike of the preeminence of the rational and the analytic in his contemporaries and in himself lurks an inner ambivalence. On the one hand, he has a powerful sense of individuality, of "myself" over against another, whose attributes one sees in derivation from oneself, in the radical acquisitiveness of the desiring mind. But at the same time there is something else at work which causes him to try to circumvent such acquisitiveness, to try to escape the entaglements of "myself" as author and only model of life.[9]

Lawrence intuited, many years before poets began to give it the attention it now enjoys, a function of the unconscious that seems to resolve the dualism between man and nature. The unconscious, in this view, is objectified and places itself between man and nature. Robert Bly calls this being the "third presence," and it is this "third presence" that Lawrence attempts to reveal in poems and fiction.[10] Hence an epiphany poem such as "The White Horse":

> The youth walks up to the white horse, to put
>   its halter on
> and the horse looks at him in silence.
> They are so silent they are in another world.[11]

Hence also derives the apocalyptic moment in the fiction—the sudden, irrationally understood revelation coming from the unconscious as well as from the writer's desire to reach for the expression of human meetings from a place beyond personality. From this, finally, comes his need to move away from his own self-centeredness, from the purloining of experience by personality, as he strives to seek out a reality more true to the "third presence" through the contemplation of icons: the Holy Ghost, the Morning Star, the forked flame.

Lawrence expresses with painful intensity in "New Heaven and Earth" a weariness with the self's authorization of its world.

I was so weary of the world,
I was so sick of it,
everything was tainted with myself,
skies, trees, flowers, birds, water,
people, houses, streets, vehicles, machines,
nations, armies, war, peace-talking,
work, recreation, governing, anarchy,
it was all tainted with myself, I knew it
all to start with
because it was all myself.[12]

In the poem's narrative, the self-weariness is transformed through a kind of psychic death. The poet finds himself remade, through mysterious alchemy; all is new and strange, and he is absolved from responsibility for its being. This is a fairly early poem, but throughout his life Lawrence wrestled with the matter of self-knowledge and submission to the innovative wind from the unknown self. In a late poem, "Terra Incognita," Lawrence describes this sense of vast possibility as "the humming of unseen harps / we know nothing of, within us." To actualize the newness, he says, we must

escape the barbed-wire enclosure
of *Know Thyself,* knowing we can never know,
we can but touch, and wonder, and ponder, and make
our effort
and dangle in a last fastidious fine delight
as the fuchsia does, dangling her reckless drop
of purple after so much putting forth
and slow mounting marvel of a little tree.[13]

To the end Lawrence struggled to gain wider acceptance of his beliefs, to change people's lives through his writing. But at the same time as he was working on his *Pansies,* poison darts directed against a corrupt society, at the same time as he was writing letters filled with bitterness and disillusion, his fiction came to possess a new quality. "Sun," *Lady Chatterley's Lover, The Man Who Died*—these works are less combative in tone, and carry a resonance distinctive among Lawrence's novels and stories. They are not less polemical, but they are less insistent; they are not less powerful in imagery, but the images are dwelt on with meditative attention.

It will not do, then, to criticize *Lady Chatterley's Lover*—as certain critics have done[14]—on the grounds that it exhibits a certain dullness, "a weary prose"—in Harry T. Moore's phrase—"only mildly chromatic." On the contrary, in this late novel Lawrence achieves an inner sureness of belief, with a letting go of self striving, that lends to the novel a calmness, a delight, and a certain acceptance of evil: a tone which, though far removed from mere tolerance, lacks the fierce denunciatory rage of earlier writings.

This quieter fictional mood is presaged by an unfinished work written after *The Plumed Serpent,* in the spring of 1925: "The Flying Fish." In this narrative, which he found himself finally unable to complete, Lawrence describes the voyage of Gethin Day, a convalescent returning home from Mexico to his ancestral seat in the English Midlands, Daybreak. The parallel with the writer's own situation is evident. Gethin Day is going back to his family home, but he feels that he is also, in some way, returning home to himself, that he is beginning to, as it were, "fall into himself." He has discovered in Mexico, through studying the hopeless, uncaring attitude of the native people, and in his sickness, that the fabric of his reality has disintegrated: the things that had mattered to him matter no longer. Fearfully he realizes that he must attend to another reality more primal than that with which he had formerly trafficked. The old consciousness, the old day, "had cracked like some great bubble, and to his uneasiness and terror, he had seemed to see through the fissures the deeper blue of that other Greater Day where moved the other sun shaking its dark blue wings."[15]

For Gethin Day the apocalypse is happening; he walks about in the era of the Last Days before the Second Coming. Sick at heart, he ponders an ancient family text, the Book of Days, "a sort of secret family Bible." Here he discovers the symbols of his own soul.

"And the time will come at last when the walls of the little day shall fall, and what is left of the family of men shall find themselves outdoors in the Greater Day, houseless and abroad, even here between the knees of the Vales, even in Crichdale. It is a doom that will come upon tall men. And then they will breathe deep, and be breathless in the great air, and salt sweat will stand on their brow thick as buds on sloe-bushes when the sun comes back. And little men will shudder and die out, like clouds of grasshoppers falling in the sea. Then tall men will remain alone in the land, moving deeper in the Greater Day, and moving deeper" ("Flying Fish," p. 785).

He begins to understand that the wanderings with which he had filled his life hitherto had been at least in part an escape from himself. His restlessness corresponds to the leap of the flying fish according to the image of the Book of Days:

"For it is on wings of fear, sped from the mouth of death, that the flying fish riseth twinkling in the air, and rustles in astonishment silvery through the thin small day. But he dives again into the great peace of the deeper day, and under the belly of death, and passes into his own.... But thy flight is not far, and thy flying is not long. Thou art a fish of the timeless Ocean, and must needs fall back. Take heed lest thou break thyself in the fall! For death is not in dying, but in the fear. Cease then the struggle of thy flight, and fall back into the deep element where death is and is not, and life is not a fleeing away. It is a beauteous thing to live and to be alive. Live then in the Greater Day, and let the waters carry thee, and the flood bear thee along, and live, only, live, no more of this hurrying away" ("Flying Fish," pp. 786, 788).

As the ship moves through the Gulf of Mexico, Day, sitting in the ship's bow, watches the clear water and the silver flying fish, whose visitation illuminates his reading of the symbols in the Book of Days. In an instant the fish rise out of the silvery water, leap, and are gone beneath the green ocean. It is a brilliant and wonderful sight. Day is transfixed, rapt in the moment of the flying fish and the ocean's green depths. It seems as if the ship will cleave forever the still water, and the flying fish will forever leap in their silver flight, a moment, then gone again swallow-like into the ocean, without a sound. In wonder he watches them fly "with wings made of pure water flapping with great speed, and long-shafted bodies of translucent silver like squirts of living water" ("Flying Fish," p. 793). He begins to find the inner peace that he had lacked, as he contemplates the ever-changing, eternal moment of the flying fish.

His delight is intensified when, a little later, a school of dolphins appears ahead of the ship. Beneath the water they perform an effortless dance that enchants Day in its harmonious unity of purpose, the dolphins continually changing places with one another as they swim—perfectly balanced, perfectly in accord, playful and seemingly laughing at their endless game. Day reflects on the consummate realization of life that is the dolphins' joyous dance, a sense of harmony unknown to man.

> No wonder Ocean was still mysterious, when such red hearts beat in it! No wonder man, with his tragedy, was a pale and sickly thing in comparison! What civilization will bring us to such a pitch of swift laughing togetherness as these fish have reached? ("Flying Fish," p. 795).

Later, Lawrence discovered such a civilization, albeit only fragments from its past, when he visited the burial grounds of the ancient Etruscans in the spring of 1927. Wall paintings on their tombs depicted scenes from Etruscan life; and in these Lawrence detected a quality of being that was infused with that sense of joyful play which he had seen in the dolphins' sport. Gethin Day is filled with wonder and delight at this unsought manifestation of the Greater Day; for, like his family treatise, it brings him home to himself.

To the dolphins' insouciance, but not their apparent joy, has come the protagonist of Lawrence's short story "The Man Who Died,"[16] as he ventures once more into the world of men. Wakening from the tomb, as Gethin Day had risen from an all but mortal sickness, the man who died (no doubt the Jesus of the Gospels) goes out, deeply disillusioned, into a world that he repudiates: the "little day" described in "The Flying Fish." Like Day, he has come to understand the world of man as caught up in a "strange entanglement of passions and circumstances and compulsion."[17] He divines that this universal bullying derives from the fear of death. "Men and women alike were mad with the egoistic fear of their own nothingness" (*Man Who Died*, p. 22). The peasant's wife, for instance, with whom he lodges, wishes thus to "possess" him.

He himself in his former mission as preacher and savior had sought to coerce men into a desired course of action.

Once a man of many words, he now resolves to "wander the world and say nothing," renouncing the effort of salvation in favor of the physician's art, since he believes that at last he has cast off his striving self. Thus, uncaring, he is freed to contemplate the various life burgeoning around him. He is no longer limited by the bounds of his morality, which compelled a certain function and unity upon creation. Now, in order to inherit the earth, he must wander alone watching "the stirring of all things among themselves." He does not strive to impose upon them a moral structure. "A sermon is so much more likely to cake into mud, and to close the fountains, than is a psalm or a song" (*Man Who Died*, p. 20). The man who died, resurrected to a new teleology, begins to see at last that, in the words of a poem by Gary Snyder, "the end is, / grace—ease— / healing / not saving."[18]

Yet newly reborn and sick with disillusion, "Jesus" lies in the peasant's yard and reflects on the deadly life of the world, and his own part in it. Then, as he watches spring unfold in sunshine and warmth, the fig tree flame into leaf, the challenge of the crowing cock, indomitable though tied by the leg, he becomes aware of "the vast resoluteness of life." Wavering between the courage of life and the will to death, he resolves that the doom of death "is a shadow compared with the raging destiny of life" (*Man Who Died*, p. 11). We are reminded of Birkin, who, near despair, discovers within himself the spark of faith that responds to Ursula's trust. *The Man Who Died* continues the dialectic of belief and disillusion, the exploration of the dual inner rivers of life and dissolution, which Lawrence struggles with through *Women in Love,* "The Reality of Peace," and *The Plumed Serpent.* At least a resolution, at least a temporary stay, is found in the precarious courage of life enacted in *Lady Chatterley's Lover* and stated explicitly in the essay "The Reality of Peace":

> If, in our heart of hearts, we can find one spark of happiness that is absolved from strife, then we are converted to the new life the moment we accept this spark as the treasure of our being. . . . If we will have a new creation on earth, if our souls are chafing to make a beginning, if our fingers are itching to start the new work of building up a new world, a whole new world with a new open sky above us, then we are transported across the unthinkable chasm from the old dead way to the beginning of all that is to be.[19]

So the man who died, barely choosing "the everlasting resoluteness of life" over the destiny of death, wanders the world in a bleak solitude like that of the protagonist of "The Man Who Loved Islands," a short story written the autumn before *The Man Who Died,* in 1926. The islander finally decides for death, but the man who died, in his solitude, yet seeks the true *eros,* the "woman who can lure my risen body, yet leave me my aloneness" (*Man Who Died,* p. 20).

Lawrence was unable to complete "The Flying Fish," for its end was to concern life in a regenerated world, the image of the greater Day—as he told the Brewsters—and he found himself incapable (he said) of conceiving such a world. He could not find the narrative images needed to complete that fragment, but he later describes some of the constituents of the life of the Greater Day in the parabolic action of *The Man Who Died.*

The Egyptian temple of Isis stands at the threshold of entrance to the Greater Day; it is encircled by the petty squabbling life of the mundane world. As "Jesus" muses on the plight of the old world, he finds that "unless we encompass it in the greater day, and set the little life in the circle of the greater life, all is disaster" (*Man Who Died,* p. 36).

Nor does entrance to the greater day need comprehension; it requires awakening: "It needs newness" (*Man Who Died,* p. 42). In the solitude of his indifference, the physician finds himself healed by surrender to the tenderness of the priestess of Isis; her physical warmth, her pristine candor, "like the heart of a rose, like the core of a flame." He realizes that he had, in his former spiritual life, desired only discarnate love: the love, he believes now, of corpses.

> "I wanted them to love with dead bodies. If I had kissed Judas with live love, perhaps he would never have kissed me with death. Perhaps he loved me in the flesh, and I willed that he should love me bodylessly" (*Man Who Died,* p. 41).

As he awakens to the physical reality of touch, the world is reborn for him to a splendor beyond "the littleness and meaningless and pain" (*Man Who Died,* p. 38). So "Jesus" reflects after their lovemaking, looking at "the vivid stars before dawn, as they rained down to the sea, and the dog-star green towards the sea's rim,"

> "How plastic it is, how full of curves and folds like an invisible rose of dark-petalled openness that shows where the dew touches its darkness! How full it is, and great beyond all gods. How it leans around me, and I am part of it, the great rose of Space. I am like a grain of its perfume, and the woman is a grain of its beauty. Now the world is one flower of many petalled darknesses, and I am in its perfume as in a touch" (*Man Who Died,* p. 44).

It is the momentary eternal reality of peace:

> There is a transfiguration, a rose with glimmering petals, upon a bush that knew no more than the dusk of green leaves heretofore. There is a new heaven on the earth, there is new heaven and new earth, the heaven and earth of the perfect rose.[20]

The expression of such delicate sensuality is a difficult task, requiring the utmost faith and attention on the part of the writer, corresponding indeed to the faith and attention required of the protagonist in the surrender of his disillusioned self to "allow that which is perfectly [himself] to take place in

[him]." As we have observed in the narrative of *The Plumed Serpent,* such scenes may devolve into the pretentious and the *faux-naif.* But, excepting perhaps one moment of mishap, Lawrence succeeds in creating the physical encounter between "Jesus" and the priestess of Isis with directness, power, and a certain splendor.[21]

He achieves success in his description of the encounter of Jesus and Isis partly by reason of the parabolic form of the narrative. The traditional associations of Isis and Osiris, and of the story of Jesus, lend a sense of largeness to the fable. So also does the writer's characterization of the priestess as the Woman Clothed with the Sun, as was Kate (to more limited effect) in *The Plumed Serpent.* However, in the parabolic narrative of *The Man Who Died* Lawrence allowed himself a more complete conventionalizing of the woman. Her temple faces the sun; she wears a saffron cloak; she is perceived by "Jesus" as having the "westering sun on her netted hair"; he ponders "the soft blue sun of her eyes" (*Man Who Died,* pp. 33, 34). Especially characteristic is the quality of sun-like warmth that "Jesus" finds in her presence.

> The woman of Isis was lovely to him, not so much in form, as in the wonderful womanly glow of her. Suns beyond suns had dipped her in mysterious fire, the mysterious fire of a potent woman, and to touch her was like touching the sun. Best of all was her tender desire for him, like sunshine, so soft and still (*Man Who Died,* p. 38).

It is the warmth of the woman's sun which heals him as the coming of dawn: he finds "a new sun ... coming up in him, in the perfect inner darkness of himself" (*Man Who Died,* p. 42).

Besides conventionalizing the protagonists, Lawrence creates a narrative which is spacious and dignified in tone, using an archaic diction that came naturally to him from his familiarity with the Bible. This is combined with a rhythmic power that creates overall a sense of winter splendor—the strength of the Southern sun—but with it a leanness.

> The wind came cold and strong from inland, from the invisible snows of Lebanon. But the temple, facing south and west, towards Egypt, faced the splendid sun of winter as he curved down towards the sea, the warmth and radiance flooded in between the pillars of painted wood. But the sea was invisible, because of the trees, though its dashing sounded among the hum of pines. The air was turning golden to afternoon. The woman who served Isis stood in her yellow robe, and looked up at the steep slopes coming down to the sea, where the olive-trees silvered under the wind like water splashing. She was alone save for the goddess. And in the winter afternoon the light stood erect and magnificent off the invisible sea, filling the hills of the coast (*Man Who Died,* pp. 22-23).

The scene within the temple, in which the priestess massages the body of the man who died, drawing him to life, is likewise taut and rhythmical, bringing into being the vitality it describes.

In silence, she softly rhythmically chafed the scar with oil. Absorbed now in her priestess's task, softly, softly gathering power, while the vitals of the man howled in panic. But as she gradually gathered power, and passed in a girdle round him to the opposite scar, gradually warmth began to take the place of the cold terror, and he felt: "I am going to be warm again, and I am going to be whole!" (*Man Who Died*, p. 42).

Equally powerful and sensuous are many of the descriptive passages— that of the nocturnal bloom of the lotus, of the fig tree bursting into leaf, the vigorous description of the wooden temple facing the winter sun. There is, too, a delicacy of tone in the writer's description of the priestess contemplating the sleeping wanderer as he lies in her goat cave; or in a later scene when, newly born to desire, he pries shellfish from the rocks, eating them with "relish and wonder for the simple taste of the sea" (*Man Who Died*, p. 33).

Yet, for all its strength and spare beauty, the narrative has a certain coldness: the winter leanness of the parable. In spite of himself the man who died must ask a last question concerning the world: "For what and to what could this infinite whirl be saved?" (*Man Who Died*, p. 22). Lawrence yearns for salvation still, as he contemplates the seeming wreckage of his own culture; and must address the "infinite whirl" directly, through exploration of the world of his own people, in the country of his deepest affection and pain, the Midlands of his boyhood.

Lawrence returned to Derbyshire briefly in 1925, then again in the summer of 1926. During that autumn he began, in Italy, from the Villa Mirenda in Scandicci, the first writing of a novel set in England that was to be *Lady Chatterley's Lover*.

In *John Thomas and Lady Jane* Lawrence discusses the time in which Connie Chatterley lives (the time in which "the cataclysm had fallen") as the period between the Resurrection and the Ascension; the men who suffered through the late war are seen as analogous to Christ before his ascension: the imagined time, in fact, of *The Man Who Died*.

How terrible the story of Jesus! It was the epitome of the story of all men. They had all been crucified, these men: all except Jack, who had balked it. But Clifford and Tommy Dukes and even Winterslow, they had all been killed, in some subtle way. And it was the strange, dim, grey era of the resurrection, with them, before the ascension into new life (*John Thomas*, p. 62).

The idea is made less of, but is implicit in the final version of the novel, in the speculations of Tommy Dukes concerning the new age of the resurrected body, the democracy of touch, which will come about when "we've shoved the cerebral stone away a bit, the money and the rest" (*LCL*, p. 86).

Typologically speaking, this is the time of the tribulations before the coming of Christ, the Last Judgment and the foundation of new heaven and earth: the apocalyptic time of disaster and death, preparatory to the final resurrection. Connie, like the priestess of Isis, waits for the reborn man, the one who has had the strength to cast aside the death shroud, the disillusioning or brutalizing of the psyche that the war has brought to those who were in any way a part of it: Clifford, Tommy Dukes, Michaelis. Life has withdrawn from their world, and their existence is an ugly and meaningless dream, "the strange grey era" of the Resurrection, before the Ascension.

In *The Rainbow,* Lawrence had expressed dissatisfaction with the scant attention paid the phenomenon of the Ascension by orthodox Christianity, as well as with the bodiless and deathly nature of the post-Resurrection events in the narrative of the life of Jesus. In this early novel he intimates the era discussed in *Lady Chatterley's Lover* and *The Man Who Died,* that of the resurrected body. His speculations are designed to offer an alternative understanding of the resurrection, one which counters traditional insistence on the preeminence of death in the Christian cycle.

> Alas, that a risen Christ has no place with us! Alas, that the memory of the passion of Sorrow and Death and the Grave holds triumph over the pale fact of Resurrection!
> But why? Why shall I not rise with my body whole and perfect, shining with strong life?... Is heaven impatient for me, and bitter against this earth, that I should hurry off, or that I should linger pale and untouched? Is the flesh which was crucified become as poison to the crowds in the street, or is it as a strong gladness and hope to them, as the first flower blossoming out of the earth's humus? (*Rainbow,* pp. 279-80).

Clifford clings tenaciously to an entropic belief in the universe as physically wasting away while spiritually ascending; he understands the body as a crude vehicle for the spirit, destined in the amelioration of the species for gradual extinction. Connie, on the other hand, argues for the greater potentiality of the physical body, which is only now beginning to come to life, only now "really rising from the tomb" as a "lovely, lovely life in the lovely universe, the life of the human body" (*LCL,* p. 282).

Though only briefly discussed in the final version of the novel, the idea of the spiritualizing of the physical, the new age of the resurrected body, had long intrigued Lawrence. Writing to Carter in June 1923 of the physical meanings of some of the symbols of Revelation, he speculates on the narrative sequence as representing "a conquest, one by one, of the lower affective centres by the mind," the New Jerusalem being "the mind enthroned." This, he says, initiated the age of the Logos in which we live and which, in its decadence, is ready for renewal, "with the polarity downward."[22] The narrative of *Lady Chatterley's Lover* explores some of the possibilities of such an age, bringing into being the notions entertained by Dukes: the resurrection of the body, the democracy of touch.

Lawrence's portrayal of post-war England is as an era physically analogous to the time of the crucifixion. The inner dialogue within this temporal framework can be seen as a debate concerning action, inner and outer, as deriving from the necessities of circumstances governing one's destiny; the directives of inner character; and that power of healing which cannot be deliberately called into being, or explained: "Not I, not I, but the wind that blows through me." The dialogue corresponds to Pascal's triad "the motions of grace, hardness of heart; external circumstances."[23]

Clifford, for example, is both victim and unpitiable oppressor. Lawrence invokes sympathy for him as a subject of the war's brutality, and as inevitably suffering the sick disillusion of the aftermath of war. The writer speaks of a corresponding indifference to hope among the miners:

> It was the bruise of the war that had been in abeyance, slowly rising to the surface and creating the great ache of unrest, and stupor of discontent. The bruise was deep, deep, deep ... the bruise of the false inhuman war. It would take many years for the living blood of the generations to dissolve the vast black clot of bruised blood, deep inside their souls and bodies. And it would need a new hope (*LCL,* pp. 56-57).

This image of trauma curiously brings to mind the nature of Lawrence's own physical sickness, so much a symptom of emotional suffering during and after the war; it is the shock of such a blow that helps to establish a settled emotional paralysis in Clifford. Dimly Connie realizes

> one of the great laws of the human soul, that when the emotional soul receives a wounding shock, which does not kill the body, the soul seems to recover as the body recovers. But this is only appearance. It is really only the mechanism of the re-assumed habit. Slowly, slowly the wound to the soul begins to make itself felt, like a bruise, which only slowly deepens its terrible ache, till it fills all the psyche (*LCL,* pp. 55-56).

Affectively he is dead to his world, his emotions a simulacrum of real bodily sympathy; and Connie feels his empty hopelessness spread to her own soul as she talks with him of his work, or of bearing a child: the phantasmagoria of a living future. There is much sympathy for Clifford's suffering under the blows of circumstance.

But he creates his own destiny. His paralysis is the manifestation of a coldness of heart that had been his even before the war.[24] Connie realizes that Clifford had always lacked vital connection with his world. He uses his class superiority, for instance, to shield him from any involvement in the lives of his workmen; and his affection for Connie is a matter of gentlemanly correctness, rather than the expression of physical warmth. For Lawrence believes that *eros* is manifested variously: it is not restricted to genital expression, but on the contrary is to be discovered in more pervasive context.

> You know I always uphold, it is the sheer physical flow which is the healing and sustaining flow to the height, it is sex, true sensual sex. But it has a thousand forms, and can even be only a mere flow in the air, to be enough.[25]

The short story "Sun," for example, in brilliant and daring imagery, embodies Lawrence's belief in the "cosmic carnality" of what he calls elsewhere the "myriad sun in chaos,"[26] as it exists in real reciprocity with the inner self in "a terrific embrace"; splendid, awesome, procreative.

So, in "Sun," Juliet's emotional self, as well as her body, is warmed by the sun's stream within her, till she becomes aware of moving into a different way of life, sensual at the core; a life like that of blind Maurice in "The Blind Man," whose sensuality threatens his sighted friend's carapace of reserve. Maurice discovers Bertie through touch, and demands the same of him—that he explore through feeling skin and scars, the blind man's ravaged face. For Maurice such bodily knowledge is the only way to find the closest and most unreserved friendship: "Oh my God, we shall know each other now, shan't we. We shall know each other now."[27] But Bertie, caught in the "little creation of the Logos," is devastated by the certainties of touch; on his return from the encounter, he reminds Isobel of a mollusc whose shell has been broken and who is now helpless.

Clifford, too, has what has been called "the shellfishness of selfishness." Cold, attentive, and correct toward his associates, his demeanor masks a pulpy interior which grows ever more flaccid within him as the carapace of his effective life in the business world becomes tougher. Like his counterpart in *Women in Love,* Gerald Crich, the more powerful Clifford becomes in the world, the more his inner psyche disintegrates. Crich, unable to tolerate his father's slow dying, finds his emotional self like a hollow shell inside which "was all the dark and fearful space of death," and which, without Gudrun's support, "would collapse upon the great dark void which circled at the centre of his soul" (*WIL,* p. 314). Clifford, likewise, becoming more powerful as an innovative mineowner, reminds Connie of a creature

> with a hard, efficient shell of an exterior and a pulpy interior, one of the amazing crabs and lobsters of the modern, industrial and financial world, invertebrates of the crustacean order, with shells of steel, like machines, and inner bodies of soft pulp (*LCL,* pp. 128-29).

But whereas, for Crich, the moment is still open for radical change, Clifford has already chosen the river of dissolution; Lawrence does not allow us to see in him the possibility of renovation.

Clifford's attachment to Connie is one of fearful acquisitiveness, which clutches to itself the talisman that will ward off death awhile; it may be the procuring of material goods, or the gathering to oneself of other persons—or of virtue: the egotism of doing good.

> The individual, the company, the nation, they are alike all possessed with one insanity, the insanity of conceit, the mania of the swollen ego. The individual, in his normal insanity, wants to swell up his ego bigger and bigger, at any cost. He must be bigger than he is. So he

fights and fights and fights to get rich, or to get on. .... It is a vast disease, and seems to be the special disease of our civilisation or our epoch. If you haven't got the disease, you are abnormal. You have to have the malady in some form or other: either the fearsome clawing tyranny of "love" and "goodness," which is the horrible clawing attempt to get some victim into the clutches of your own egotistic love, your own egoistic virtue, your own egoistic way of salvation; or you have the less high-minded, more ignoble but perhaps not so deadly clutch-clutch-clutch after money and success. The disease grows as a cancer grows, ever extending its clutch (*John Thomas,* pp. 99-100).

Such death-fearing lust for possession seems to be endemic in the world as it is viewed by "Jesus" in *The Man Who Died;* it is the Little Day, which he escapes through the unpossessive delight and surrender of his love for the priestess of Isis. This is the little world, too, which Gethin Day flees, the contrast to which he finds in the insouciant delight of the dolphins who swim together in changing harmony "enjoying one laugh of life" ("Flying Fish," p. 794).

The joy of the Greater Day is unknown to Clifford, whose stranglehold on life causes him not only to maintain a tenacious grip on his wife and to bully his subordinates, but also to imagine himself unharmed by the future. Hence his abstract talk of an heir to Wragby, his concern for the perpetuation of a dominant aristocracy, the desperate Platonism that is so marked a part of his character in *John Thomas and Lady Jane* (less so in *Lady Chatterley's Lover,* which is altogether less prolific of discussion). Having so anxious a hold on the present, he is obsessed by the need for immortality. Connie for her part grows to understand the reverse case more fully—that, as Blake puts it, "Eternity is in love with the productions of time"; or, in Lawrence's words,

A flower passes, and that perhaps is the best of it. If we can take it in its transience, its breath, its maybe mephistophelian, maybe palely ophelian face, the look it gives, the gesture of its full bloom, and the way it turns upon us to depart—that was the flower, we have had it, and no *immortelle* can give us anything in comparison . . . merely the breath of the moment, and one eternal moment easily contradicting the next eternal moment.[28]

The pansy's momentary fragrance is the more lovely in that it contains the smell of the humus of decayed matter from which it sprung.

Clifford, then, embodies that egotistic, death-driven will to power, attention to which comes at the expense of that paid to the emotional self, which then, undernourished, etiolates and will finally perish. The destruction that he has witnessed and himself suffered during the war accounts in part for his emotional sickness. But Lawrence holds him responsible for his inner disintegration, and therefore responsible for the disintegration of his society and environment: the barren and brutal lives of the miners, the ugliness of Teborshall and gloom of Wragby, the denaturing industrialism of the area, which debilitates the affective lives of those who are subject to it. The aesthetic brutality of Tevershall is directly related to Clifford's hardness of heart. "You don't give one heartbeat of real sympathy," Connie says to Clifford.

> "And besides, who has taken away from the people their natural life and manhood, and given them this industrial horror? Who has done that?"
> "And what must I do?" he asked, green. "Ask them to come and pillage me?"
> "Why is Tevershall so ugly, so hideous? Why are their lives so hopeless?"
> "They built their own Tevershall, that's part of their display of freedom. They built themselves their pretty Tevershall, and they live their own pretty lives. I can't live their lives for them. Every beetle must live its own life."
> "But you make them work for you. They live the life of your coal mine."
> "Not at all. Every beetle finds its own food. Not one man is forced to work for me."
> "Their lives are industrialized and hopeless, and so are ours," she cried (*LCL,* p. 217).

As she contemplates the squalor of Tevershall and its dreary environs, devoid of any gladness or sensitivity, the outward manifestation of a people whose intuitive faculties have atrophied, Connie is horrified at the thought of bearing a child to such a world. It would be born on the one hand to an environment created in the form of a people subdued to the debased medium of their lives: coal face or ironworks. On the other hand, her child must contend, too, with the power of the industrial owners, who clasp to themselves their isolating birthright of aristocratic prerogative. It is indeed the time of tribulation, the era of *noli me tangere* before the dawn of the Resurrection.

> There, in the world of the mechanical, greedy, greedy mechanism and mechanised greed, sparkling with lights and gushing hot metal and roaring with traffic, there lay the vast evil thing, ready to destroy whatever did not conform. Soon it would destroy the wood, and the bluebells would spring no more. All vulnerable things must perish under the rolling and running of iron (*LCL,* p. 140).

An example, perhaps on a small scale, of such destruction is enacted in a scene that vividly describes the relation between the industrialist and his subordinates, man and environment alike being subjected to his self-aggrandizing will. During an excursion into the wooded part of the estate, Clifford's mechanical wheelchair breaks down. Instead of relying patiently on the help offered by Connie and Mellors, Clifford, in a passion of frustration, tries to force the machine into action. In his infuriated efforts he flattens bluebells and anemones as his chair lurches back and forth. Finally, unable to master the machine, he asks the keeper to try to start it going. Clifford bullies him verbally and at length forces him to push the heavy vehicle beyond his strength. Clifford himself is unaware that Mellors has been overtaxed by the physical effort; he makes it his business not to notice such things. But Connie is enraged by her husband's lack of feelings towards his keeper. It is an occasion typical of Clifford's way of imposing himself on the world; and Lawrence finds it paradigmatic of the greedy mind bent to master the world through its technological manipulation, but finally subject to its instrument, the machine, which subdues that mind to its own mode of being. Clifford, paralyzed in his physical psyche, mashing the bluebells in his frenzy to control the vehicle, forcing his servant to the point of near collapse as he lifts the heavy weight of master and chair; Clifford disregarding the keeper's pain, inattentive to the decencies of fellow feeling and the expression of gratitude—it is, as Connie says, a disgusting performance.

I have touched on some of the differences between the early and the published versions of *Lady Chatterley's Lover,* in particular a reduction in the third version of the lengthy discussions and psychological analyses that are characteristic of *John Thomas and Lady Jane;* the published novel finds its meaning more consistently through action and image. Evidently in the first and second versions "saving," not "healing," was uppermost in Lawrence's mind. As he revised, he concentrated on the restorative power of the relationship, rather than on social criticism. In the earlier versions, Parkin is a man of the people only, with little experience of the middle or upper classes. There is a great deal of talk about social differences between Connie and Parkin, and Connie and Clifford, as well as a wonderfully developed confrontation between Connie and Parkin's working-class friends, the Tewsons, in a scene of devastating realism. There is talk of Bolshevism, and the precarious hold of the masters on the populace; a sense of the imminence of political revolution is in the air.

There is, too, much personal discussion between Connie and Parkin, who is sexually as well as socially quite unsophisticated; he and she talk about their feelings for each other in realistic psychological fashion. A much larger proportion of the novel is taken up with matters of external circumstance, the logistical arrangements attendant upon an affair, particularly one so discrepant in social standing. The scenes which take place in the wood, especially the lovemaking between Connie and Parkin, are underdeveloped when compared with the later version.

It is not only the focus of relationship between Connie and Mellors which shifts away from social concerns in the third version; other characters are also seen in different perspective. In *The First Lady Chatterley* Duncan has a fairly prominent role in the latter part of the narrative, as Connie's sympathetic friend and confidant—a fact which again contributes to the psychological realism of the earlier versions. Hilda, in the first version, is a more sympathetic character, much like Connie, an ally for her. No mention is made of Michaelis until the third version. By revising the portrayal of Duncan to make him a less attractive person, in fact a representative of the atomistic and sterile culture, his art effete and mechanical; by representing Hilda, likewise, as the modern woman, self-sufficient and assertive, Lawrence points up the precariousness, the vulnerability of Connie's venture into the new life, surrounded as she is with the defeated, the hopeless, the corrupt. Michaelis is drawn as representative of a final expression of the culture's degeneration. Although Connie responds to a certain beauty of melancholy in Michaelis, she is unable to love in hopelessness; and he in his disillusion remains as he wishes, essentially isolated in the *noli me tangere* of the unascended body.

Lawrence makes Mellors a former commissioned officer in the war, and therefore he is able to move with some ease between social worlds. Lawrence thus manages, in the third version of his novel, to deflect attention from the matter of social standing; for he realizes that this is not essentially his subject. He develops the scenes of lovemaking which proceed with increasingly greater understanding and intensity between the lovers. He expands the scenes in which Connie explores the wood, both before and after she meets the keeper. In short, he concentrates on various forms of erotic encounter and the radical inner changes effected by these—the rebirth of Connie to an understanding of matter as "succinct with spirit": the resurrection of the world's body. These manifestations are in the novel the motions of grace; "the end is, / grace— ease— / healing, / not saving."

Thus the structure of the novel offers itself as a mandala of contemplation, exploring external circumstances, the hardness of the heart, and the spirit of grace. The beginning treats primarily of external circumstances and hardness of heart. Then, in the course of the narrative, we move into the inner circle, the spirit of grace, in the exploration of the tenderness of physical love in Connie and Mellors. These scenes are structurally at the center of the novel. Towards the end we move out again to the outer circle—the question of circumstance— but now in scenes infused with our understanding (as with Connie's) of the motions of grace, revaluing willfulness and accident.

Much of the early part of the novel is expository, recapitulating Connie's and Clifford's former life, setting the scene for Connie's awakening. The conversations, for example, between Clifford and his cronies introduce ideas— through Tommy Dukes, a sort of "John the Baptist" to Mellors—that stir her consciousness, in their outline of the notion of the resurrected body. Such scenes of exposition and static dialogue are contrived and out of keeping, perhaps, with subsequent happenings. But Lawrence didn't much care. As Joyce Carol Oates points out in regard to the poems—her comments being equally applicable to the novels—Lawrence's writings are

fragments of a total self that could not always keep up the strain of totality. Sometimes Lawrence was anguished over this, but most of the time he believed that in his poetry, as in life itself, what must be valued is the springing forth of the natural, forcing its own organic shape, not being forced into a preordained structure.... [He is] quite maliciously willing to inform us of the dead spaces, the blanks in his imagination.... He had no interest in "perfection"; he would have scorned even the speculative idea of hoping for either a perfection in life or in art—he is too engrossed in the beauty of the natural flux.[29]

The early part of the novel reflects Lawrence's impatience to come to the heart of his argument; he sketchily delineates the necessary preliminaries. It is possible that, in spite of our lingering modernist bias towards self-consistent textural and stylistic unity in the well-wrought, finished artistic object, we also should see these scenes as sketchily as he did and attend to the *process* of art, the "quick" of the developing narrative.

There have been critics, also, who have disliked the scenes at the contemplative center of the novel. Cavitch, for instance, finds that in the successive revisions of the novel Lawrence increasingly freed his subjects from the "weight of misery and doom upon other people's lives." The lovers, he maintains, are released into the gratifying world of idyll, secure from the complications and vicissitudes of society.[30]

In those successive versions of *Lady Chatterley's Lover,* Lawrence increasingly concentrates on the passion and affection of Connie and Mellors and their finding of peace. Such moments of accord are, I maintain, the "motions of grace," which transvalue outer circumstances through altering inner address. For the faith of the visionary writer such as Lawrence is that what a sceptic sees as idyll, an illusory harmony, may be the world imaginatively renovated by a radical change in perception—enlightenment that, even if momentary, has the power to irradiate the opacities of the quotidian. This is the moment that I have throughout this study seen as Lawrence's expression of *apokalypsis.* For the visionary, confusion between the idyllic and the genuinely restorative is a product of imaginative sloth. This is not to say that the visionary sees no "idyllic" world of unearned harmony. On the contrary, Blake—to name one obvious example—saw all the difference in the world (and it was for him *in* the world) between the innocence of those unaware of inner and outer conflict and those who had incorporated into their lives the necessary world of intransigent experience, and had transformed this into the state of mind he called "organized innocence":[31] this is the world discovered by Connie and Mellors through their sensuality and affection—the attainment of the reality of peace as "the deepest desire of the soul."

Therefore it is a serious misreading of the novel to see the lovers—in the way Cavitch, among others, sees them—as free from the claims of a recalcitrant society. Much of the power of the central events of the novel lies precisely in their vulnerability and their encirclement. Connie and Mellors find peace in spite of external circumstances and hardness of heart (the lovers' own resistance as well as the opposition of those around them). Hence the rightness also of the subdued ending, Mellors's letter to Connie, as the closing expression of a relationship thoroughly responsive to the imperfect and the resistant within and without. Flame gives off its own light, but it requires the world's air to burn in. "Patience, always patience," writes Mellors. "This is my fortieth winter. And I can't help all the winters that have been. But this winter I'll stick to my little pentecost flame, and have some peace" (*LCL*, p. 364).

The sense of the circle, I have said, is a principle of the overall structure; but within individual scenes, too, there is the same sense of the circle with a still core. Ringed round with coldheartedness and the chill of separating circumstances, each episode has at its center radiant images—baby chickens, wildflowers, the tenderness of caress—icons so simple that the mind is tempted to move away in search of something of more obvious importance.

Indeed it is just this matter of importance that is lacking to Connie in her dreary round of habitual errands and duties at Wragby. "It was as if the very material you were made of was cheap stuff, and was fraying out to nothing" (*LCL*, p. 71). As she returns home from a walk in the woods, she realizes that the word "home" has no importance, but has somehow been trivialized.

> All the great words, it seemed to Connie, were cancelled for her generation: love, joy, happiness, home, mother, father, husband, all these great, dynamic words were half dead now, and dying from day to day (*LCL*, p. 70).

This is the world of matter of fact, without intrinsic interest: "the supremacy of the desert."[32] Importance, the dynamic principle of vitality which passes "from the world as one to the world as many" is no longer present to formerly powerful modes of relationship. The old morality of connection has been lost, and there is no new power to bring into being that "union of harmony, intensity, and vividness"[33] which might be able to revitalize the old pieties and bring affective life back into the ancient symbols: the vivid reality of that which is truly "there" as present to the perceiver.

It is in fact reality, rather than beauty, that is dominant in Connie's awareness of the keeper as she catches sight of him washing himself behind the cottage. What she feels, with visceral shock, is the actuality of his presence, the gathering together of his being in pure and unconscious attention. It is this "suchness" of the creature that, living as she has been like Plato's cave dwellers, strikes her with overwhelming force as the living reality. The mundane flames into importance, radiating a sense of the significance of the moment and, within this, of a new future. Possibility enters her as an impregnation; for, in Whitehead's formulation, actuality is "something that matters, by reason of its own self-enjoyment, which includes enjoyment of others and transitions towards the future."[34]

It is evident that Connie's experience of the occasion as the conjunction of transcendence and immanence in her vision of Mellors has something of the same motion as apocalyptic revelations discussed in connection with earlier novels. Lawrence understands such revelation by the paradigm of St. Paul's conversion: sudden, self-transforming, and imperfectly understood by the analyzing mind. In order for revelation to occur there must be a previous resistance, if unconscious, to the surrender of apocalypse. This is true for Ferguson, of "The Horse Dealer's Daughter," for Tom and Will Brangwen, for Birkin, and others. Connie, too, self-immured in the dream world of Wragby, finds herself overwhelmed by the shock of transforming insight.

> But with her mind she was inclined to ridicule. A man washing himself in a backyard! No doubt with evilsmelling yellow soap!—She was rather annoyed; why should she be made to stumble on these vulgar privacies? (*LCL*, p. 76).

However, this is the last of such psychic conflagrations. Gradually Connie becomes open to the surrender of herself to whatever change may be working within. We are reminded of the protagonist in "Song of a Man Who Has Come Through," who at last submits himself to the directives of the creative wind within him. When one begins to "fall into oneself," Lawrence maintains, it is through surrender to the visitation of "the primal unknown": "not of myself, but of the unknown which has ingress into me."[35] The relaxation of striving, the "falling into oneself," that directs Lawrence's later writing creates in *Lady Chatterley's Lover* that mellowing, contemplative tone which I have mentioned, and it causes him also to have no further need of apocalypse. There is no need to throw oneself on the consuming pyre, to rise remade, for the lambent flame flickers where it will through creation: "I do but conduct the unknown of my beginning to the unknown of my end, through the transfiguration of perfect being."[36]

After her first vision of Mellors Connie is aware that something has changed in her. Hardly knowing why, she contemplates, as she has not for a long while, her naked body, realizing its devolution into apathy (as *apatheia*), the counterpart and expression of her emotional boredom. Without so articulating it, she sees her body as a contrast to that of the keeper: his, full of awareness and attention, spiritual substance; hers growing meaningless, so much insignificant matter. She blames Clifford for his indifference to simple human contact—the lack of warmth that is destroying her being, as it is chilling the world.[37] For Lawrence,

> it is in the living touch between us and other people, other lives, other phenomena that we move and have our being. Strip us of our human contacts and of our contact with the living earth and the sun, and we are almost bladders of emptiness.[38]

Half consciously, resentment against the dreariness of her life begins to grow in her, so that, without knowing why, she responds to Dukes's speculations concerning the "democracy of touch" and the "resurrection of the body." She acquiesces in the appointment of a nurse for Clifford, finding release thereby, aware that "she breathed freer, a new phase was going to begin in her life" (*LCL,* p. 97).

And so the delicate, persistent coming-into-being of the wildflowers arouses her compassion. In the turbulent winds of March they distinguish themselves, hazel, daffodil, celandine, ineluctably pushing through the humus, sweet and cold. She is released from herself as she contemplates the strength of these uncaring manifestations of life independent of her own will, and is refreshed to think of the daffodils dipping silently through the long, cold night, meeting darkness and sunlight, but growing and coming to themselves in their own manner and with their proper timeliness.

The spring which she visits the following day—St. Johns Well—reveals itself likewise in clarity, not as the symbolized nature of Clifford's "literary" imagination but manifesting the "self-importance" of its own suchness.

> It was cold on this hillside, and not a flower in the darkness of larches. But the icy little spring softly pressed upwards from its tiny well-bed of pure, reddish-white pebbles. How icy and clear it was! brilliant!... She heard the faint tinkle of water, as the tiny overflow trickled over and down hill. Even above the hissing boom of the larchwood, that spread its bristling, leafless, wolfish darkness on the downslope, she heard the tinkle as of tiny water-bells (*LCL,* p. 100).

The spring matters in the reality of its own being—as Mellors, washing himself, had impressed her in the candor of the creature perfectly present to itself, and self-expressing.

Refreshed, Connie discovers then the quiet clearing in the woods where the growing pheasants are reared: the keeper's domain. Mellors himself is instinctively aware of a subdued sadness in Connie, though he resists the invasion of his privacy. As he works, Connie is reminded of her earlier sense of him. Again she sees, watching him hammer the chicken coops, the intentness of his being. "It was the stillness, and the timeless sort of patience, in a man impatient and passionate, that touched Connie's womb" (*LCL,* p. 103). To her awakened senses, he has a certain non-coercive vitality that is another manifestation, and counterpart, of the wild daffodils which had so stirred her earlier: independently they thrive in their own coming to be. In the case of the keeper, she feels that he has understood and accepted into himself a world of living beyond hers—suffering accepted, experience integrated beyond the need for assertion. "And this relieved her of herself; she felt almost irresponsible" (*LCL,* p. 103).

So time is transformed; the mechanical world of activity drops away, and she finds herself within the living flow of pure awareness. The motions of grace are revealed: for her, in the spatial mandala of the clearing of the woods; for us, in the images of the narrative.

But the moment is ringed around, as the clearing in the woods is surrounded by the encroaching industrial Midlands. The candid moment disperses; she returns to the chilly formalities of Wragby. But the moment has spoken for her. The next time she returns to the hut, she finds that the wood resonates with life.

Old oak trees stood around, grey, powerful trunks, rain-blackened, round and vital, throwing off reckless limbs. The ground was fairly free of undergrowth, the anemones sprinkled, there was a bush or two, elder, or guelder-rose, and a purplish tangle of bramble; the old russet of bracken almost vanished under green anemone ruffs (*LCL,* pp. 108-9).

Again the moment passes; she must contend with the keeper's resistance to her presence in the quiet place. But now she is awakened, and begins gradually to submit herself to the erotic reality of the living wood.

But at Wragby she must witness the demeaning power play of Clifford and Ivy Bolton: she, determined to master him through a subservient bossiness, he continually frustrating her will. It becomes apparent that Mrs. Bolton, perversely in love with Clifford, finds lurking satisfaction in the triumph of her will, as he gradually submits to the subtle assault of her regime. Together they destroy the people of Tealshall through indiscriminate gossip, vicious and humiliating in its pretense of righteousness and its rabid, gloating curiosity to uncover the last details of failure and suffering.

Clifford, desperate at the unthought loss of his own life, must shore it up with the failure and loss of others, someone else's suffering being a matter of triumph to him as proof of his own success. So it is with the "strange awful thrill" of his game shooting in autumn, an earlier expression of the frantic possession he takes of his life: for, hearing the death scream of the rabbit during shooting expeditions "he exulted curiously."

All this grasping at power—through creatures, persons, and technology—is at the expense of his emotional strength. He, like Connie, is reborn, but in ghastly parody. His new world reveals the supremacy of brute matter as instrumental to his design; whereas for Connie the material world, losing none of its physicality, yet becomes suffused with spirit as she allows herself to witness its incomprehensible destiny. As Clifford had once sucked out the life of the people he dissected in writing, so he now pillages the material world in a gathering of armaments that will, he desperately assumes, protect him against his own immanent dissolution. Now he slides into emotional impotence, his assertions of love having all the logic of truth and none of the reality.

As for Connie, her passage is toward ever greater consciousness of her life as being in reciprocal relationship with the ancient oaks, the clear spring, the young plants. She returns more and more frequently to the wood, to the vital reticence of the enduring trees and, when they are set, to the brooding hens, warm and solicitous in their nurturing office.

The unfolding of spring is "with great tufts of primroses under the hazels" and hens fluffed on their hatching eggs. Connie is affected powerfully by these appearances, in contrast to the coldhearted world outside the wood. When the first pheasant chick is born in "pure, sparky, fearless new life," she feels herself disintegrating under the pressure of her two worlds—her forlorn state at Wragby and her witness to the surge of various life thrusting into being. Sitting before the coops, she takes "the little drab thing between her hands," where it stands, "on its impossible little stalks of legs, its atom of balancing life trembling through its almost weightless feet into Connie's hands." The tiny creature breaks her defences; she begins crying "blindly, in all the anguish of her generation's forlornness" (*LCL,* pp. 134-35). It is to this vulnerability that the keeper responds, and his comfort is with the answering reality of caress.

> He laid his hand on her shoulder, and softly, gently, it began to travel down the curve of her back, blindly, with a blind stroking motion, to the curve of her crouching loins. And there his hand softly, softly stroked the curve of her flank, in the blind instinctive caress (*LCL,* pp. 135-36).

Thus a living peace is consummated between them. They enter the erotic dialogue which is that of oak sap rising through the sun-warmed tree; the maturing egg; the opening of the wet hazel bud; the daily uncurling of bracken. She is reborn to the patience and power of erotic compassion. It is

> spring in the world of the living;
> wonderment organising itself, heralding itself
> with the violets,
> stirring of new seasons.[39]

Again, the moment is as vulnerable as the awakened body. To the world of "the rolling and running of iron" they must return. We are once more aware of the movement between contemplation of the spirit of grace and the alternate reality of the heart's unbending harshness.

However, grace begins gradually to overcome the hardness of the heart. Looking at Clifford, Connie realizes—as Mellors has not realized—that the power of her husband's rapacious will is finally weaker than the energy of life in Mellors. Clifford's world, she believes, will perish, and the new world intimated by Tommy Dukes, the world of the resurrected body—the post-Ascension world—will come to pass. It is a curious and moving reversal that Connie, who originally had been comforted by the keeper, is now their source of hope. Mellors, sick in despair at the world's corruption, has little faith for a continuing life for the two of them outside their sanctuary. It is Connie who is able to penetrate and transform her outward life with the reality of her new knowledge; she goes forward, making her plans for their meeting with the outer world. Gradually, through her faith in them, she brings Mellors to her own hope.

> "Shall I tell you?" she said, looking into his face. "Shall I tell you what you have that other men don't have, and that will make the future? Shall I tell you?"
> "Tell me then," he replied.
> "It's the courage of your own tenderness... " (*LCL,* p. 334).[40]

We can read in the despondency of Mellors Lawrence's own despair. It is as if, in his melancholy and his flickering hope, Mellors expresses the author's own valiant, wavering belief in the future—the struggle as ever between allegiance to the river of life or the stream of dissolution.

It is therefore the triumph of his faith that, as we think about the novel, we consider—in the *mythos*—the narration leading to a hope for "this infinite whirl," which, if not robust, has at least a persistent glimmering. Mellors writes to Connie, in the long letter with which the novel ends, of the "little pentecost flame," saying, "I won't let the breath of people blow it out. I believe in a higher mystery, that doesn't let even the crocus be blown out" (*LCL,* p. 364).[41]

But it is especially in the *dianoia* of the novel, in the narrative as mandala, that we find the most telling aspect of the book. That which resonates most clearly, most deeply, is the center of each circle, and the center of the circular narrative: the scenes between Connie and Mellors, including the vibrating life around them, participant in the occasions of their meeting. These scenes testify to the writer's belief in the power of the awakened heart to discover importance within the matter of fact: the holiness of matter, whether it is in the lovemaking of the man and the woman, the opening of the celandine blossom, the odd, orange hair of the child, the sparky chirping of a pheasant chick. It is this which carries within it the lure of the future, the hope of the new age in which "we can but touch, and wonder, and ponder, and make our effort."

Increasingly more alive to the manifestations of eros, Connie finds the wood as she walks in it alive with its own different life, in correspondence with her own.

> It was a grey, still afternoon, with the dark-green dogs'-mercury spreading under the hazel copse, and all the trees making a silent effort to open their buds. Today she could almost feel it in her own body, the huge heave of the sap in the massive trees, upwards, up, up to the bud-tips, there to push into little flamy oak leaves, bronze as blood. It was like a tide running turgid upward, and spreading on the sky (*LCL,* p. 143).

One of the most moving expressions of this correspondence of human and natural is the scene in which Connie and Mellors adorn themselves with wildflowers, after a sexual meeting and the rain's lustration of their naked bodies. Again, what is presented is something very simple, innocent. The mind in its cynicism is tempted to denigrate, or at least disregard this expression of faith; but the emotional mind is delighted. The scene is the more powerful in that it is permeated with the presence of the world of circumstance and rigidity; we are continually aware of the vulnerability of the lovers' passion. During a gloomy discussion of the world of society, Mellors considers with some satisfaction the inevitable and imminent extinction of the human race. Connie, nevertheless, is borne up by hope, which is in part the hope of her pregnancy. Then they cast aside their talk, and let the rain wash them clean.

It is a beautiful episode, strong in images, powerfully rhythmical, with overtones of a mythological scene—the pursuit of woodnymph by satyr—but with none of the artificiality or fancifulness of literary mythologizing; this is a carnal encounter, naturally feral.

> She was nearly at the wide riding when he came up and flung his naked arm round her soft, naked-wet middle. She gave a shriek and straightened herself, and the heap of her soft, chill flesh came up against his body. He pressed it all up against him, madly, the heap of soft, chilled female flesh that became quickly warm as flame, in contact. The rain steamed on them till they smoked. He gathered her lovely, heavy posteriors one in each hand and pressed them in towards him in a frenzy, quivering motionless in the rain. Then suddenly he tipped her up and fell with her on the path, in the roaring silence of the rain, and short and sharp, he took her, short and sharp and finished, like an animal (*LCL,* p. 266).

At the same time it has the glow of the spirit's infusion, the passionate perception of the body's spiritual reality.

> She dropped her blanket and kneeled on the clay hearth, holding her head to the fire, and shaking her hair to dry it. He watched the beautiful curving drop of her haunches. That fascinated him today. How it sloped with a rich down-slope to the heavy roundness of her buttocks! And in between, folded in the secret warmth, the secret entrances!
>
> He stroked her tail with his hand, long and subtly taking in the curves and the globefulness (*LCL,* p. 267).

The muscular drive of the event leads with fine balance into the more delicately contemplative tone of the following scene, in which Mellors threads wildflowers into the brown fleece of Connie's pubic hair and she in turn adorns his with campion and forget-me-not. He then disappears into the wood to return "trotting strangely," carrying an armful of wildflowers with which he crowns "John Thomas and Lady Jane," bedecking his own penis and body hair and her breasts and navel. Playful though intent, he crowns their bodies with all the flowers of spring. The whole event, lustration and crowning, creates anew the moment of passionate tenderness between them, the surrender each to each, the balanced reciprocity of their relationship.[42]

The scene enacts, too, a notion of male and female complementarity in the masculine drive of the first episode, the chase in the rain, and the feminine occasion which follows, as they thread each other with flowers. There is a yin/yang conjunction of opposites within the action of the scene itself. Nor is the interchange solely between the human participants. Rain and wildflowers are realized with the vivid clarity of their self-subsisting part in the occasion. These natural manifestations—wood and wildflowers—form the nexus of associations within which Lawrence builds the scene as a celebration of the sacred marriage, the crowning of the King and Queen of the May. Without overt allusion, Lawrence has created the event anew, drawing from the source of such belief: the procreative vitality of the natural world. What Frazer called, with the detachment of scepticism, "homeopathic magic," Lawrence enacts as the truly sacred marriage of Connie and Mellors within their vegetative world. And as the outer life of Wragby comes into dominance again with Connie's impending vacation, the sacred marriage is consummated in a "night of sensual passion."

Much has been made by critics of this "night of sensual passion" in the course of which, evidently, the lovers engage in anal intercourse. Frank Kermode sees this event as the culmination of Connie's initiation and rebirth, according to the original plot of the Apocalypse, which Lawrence, he argues, re-enacts in the structure of *Lady Chatterley's Lover*. The ultimate purgation is a burning out of "the last and deepest recesses of organic shame."[43]

I am unable to see Kermode's seven stages of initiation, corresponding to the opening of the seven seals, with the specifically incremental enlightenment for Connie that he claims for them. More generally, it does seem to me that Connie's successive encounters with Mellors serve to deepen and intensify her passion and develop her understanding of the sensual self, including its relation to the outer world. However, in this climactic scene Lawrence's intention is to render justice also to the excremental in man, to lift an old taboo. The events of the night come to Connie as a radical and unbidden access of sensual knowledge within "the jungle of herself." As such it is indeed an apocalyptic initiation, in a "sensuality sharp and searing as fire, burning the soul to tinder." The act "stripped her to the very last, and made a different woman of her" (*LCL*, pp. 298-99).

Perhaps because the verbal description, however veiled, of such an action—revealing, literally, "the most secret places of life"—was necessarily, at the time, so deliberate an exorcism, it is hardly surprising that the writing here becomes tense, overanxious, as Lawrence, through choice, comments on the purgative act. The tone becomes shrill and assertive; the commentary is overdone. Our proper response is, it seems to me, again to attend on the essential energy of the occasion—the description of the event itself, including the foregoing ambiance of passion and hostility created by the "chemical" friability of Hilda's visit—all the collisions of forces that lead to the evening's sensual consummation.

With the departure of Connie to Venice, the narrative moves outward; the novel deals with the outer circumference of the book's *mythos*—external circumstance and hardness of heart—as Connie goes about the tortuous process of disentangling her outer life from Clifford's.

Just as Lawrence sees the crowning of Mellors and Connie with wildflowers as the celebration of the *hieros gamos,* and as Connie partakes too of the attributes of the Woman Clothed with the Sun, the Magna Mater, in allusions to the golden glow which her body seems to possess, so she is also seen by the writer as Persephone, in the regenerative phase of the threefold goddess. Like the priestess of Isis, Connie is an agent of rebirth. As she wanders the wood in March, she is associated with the springing of new vegetation, with "the breath of Persephone.... out of hell on a cold morning" (*LCL,* p. 98). Moreover, the action of *Lady Chatterley's Lover,* like that of *The Man Who Died,* moves from winter to high summer, at which time a different phase of the cycle is initiated, the time of fructive meeting being past.

This suggestion of cycle is one aspect of Lawrence's abiding concern for timeliness, which is itself a concomitant of his acceptance of the necessities of change. The fine account of the varying relationship necessary between a man and a woman in marriage, as he expresses it in "A Propos of *Lady Chatterley's Lover,*" is there linked with his belief in psychic time as inextricably meshed with the rhythms of the natural world.

> Marriage is the clue to human life, but there is no marriage apart from the wheeling sun and the nodding earth, from the straying of the planets and the magnificence of the fixed stars. Is not a man different, utterly different, at dawn from what he is at sunset? and a woman too? And does not the changing harmony and discord of their variation make the secret music of life?[44]

The Church in its wisdom preserved man's inner sense of the circadian cycle, through its establishment of the canonical hours, and the sense of periodic time by means of the various moods expressed through the rituals of religious festivals, reflecting so intimately the rhythm of the human seasons of the psyche. Lawrence's own representation of the inward rhythm of the time between Crucifixion and Ascension, which is the narrative of *Lady Chatterley's Lover,* bears witness to the acuteness with which he understood the wisdom of the ancient calendar of the church.

Acceptance of cycle implies readiness for Persephone's return to the underworld, and unwillingness to try to enforce a lingering above, a drawing out of the time, in inner or in outer season. Eventually the time of separation comes about:

> Now it is Autumn and the falling fruit
> and the long journey toward oblivion.

With the certitude of the reality of peace, the sensual fulfillment portrayed in *Lady Chatterley's Lover,* it is possible for Lawrence to go on to contemplate, in his final writings, "the last wonder," the long voyage across the dark sea.

6

Conclusion: Marriage with the Living Dark

The printing and distribution of *Lady Chatterley's Lover* during 1928 occasioned Lawrence much frustration. His typist refused to proceed with so indecent a work; the Italian-speaking printing house was ill-equipped and could not set the whole of the book at once, thus causing further delay; copies of the novel, sold by private subscription in England and America, were confiscated, suppressed, and resold at exorbitant prices; and the edition was widely pirated. At the same time, a manuscript of *Pansies,* en route to Lawrence's agent, was seized in the mail by a zealous Home Secretary, William Joynson-Hicks, who was convinced that anything issuing from the pen of the writer of *Lady Chatterley's Lover* must be obscene material. Furthermore, in July 1929, the Warren Gallery in London, where a number of Lawrence's erotic paintings were on exhibit, was raided by the police, and thirteen of his pictures removed.

All this embittered and angered Lawrence, as many of the poems in *Pansies, More Pansies,* and *Nettles* witness. "Ah the clean waters of the sky," he writes in "Give Me a Sponge."

> ah! can you wash
> away the evil starings and the breath
> of the foul ones from my pictures? Oh purify
> them now from all this touch of tainted death![1]

But at the same time as Lawrence was delivering himself of these bitter comments, a stronger countermood, which I have argued was already apparent in *Lady Chatterley's Lover* and *The Man Who Died,* finds expression in the meditative poems of the last months of his life, as the poet reflects through them on his own death. He was by then in an advanced stage of tuberculosis (though he would never call his sickness by its name). In 1927, a tuberculosis expert named Hans Carossa, who had examined Lawrence, judged that the deterioration of the lungs should already have killed him; he gave Lawrence at the most two or three years to live.

Much earlier, in *Sons and Lovers,* Lawrence had described the untimely death of Paul Morel's brother William and the profound grief it occasioned in the family, particularly in the mother. Later in the same narrative the writer describes, with almost unendurable anguish, the dying of Mrs. Morel, the euthanasia performed by Paul and Annie, and the psychic devolution suffered by Paul during the weeks and months following her death. There can be no doubt that Lawrence is in these scenes recapitulating the death of his own brother Ernest and that of his mother. In the novel these are devastating and untimely events, occasions of despair to the living.

Elsewhere in the novels, in non-autobiographical context, Lawrence creates scenes of violent and untoward death; often, however, such death is seen as a final outcome of the individual's psychic dying. This is the case with Gerald Crich, his father the industrialist, his sister Diana—all in a manner doomed by their death-like living. Physical death is the outer manifestation of an inner dissolution. Likewise Lawrence regards Ben Cooley of *Kangaroo* as far advanced in psychic disintegration; the killing of Cooley has therefore a certain terrible beauty to Somers, who craves, not the gentleness and brotherly love of Kangaroo, but the ingress of the dark gods and the silence of the intrinsic soul. The "woman who rode away" evidently journeys to the Indian village as a sacrifice, offering herself as the embodiment of a doomed white culture. All these individuals die as the psychic river of dissolution spills foaming into the sea.

But between writing the first and second versions of *Lady Chatterley's Lover* Lawrence spent some time contemplating another kind of death—that which follows a time of fulfillment: "The life on earth [has been] so good, the life below [can] not but be a continuance of it."[2] In the spring of 1927 the writer visited, with his peaceful Buddhist friend Earl Brewster, the various decayed Etruscan tombs near the Tyrrhenian coast of Italy. He wrote about his findings in a series of essays, *Etruscan Places*.

The narrative of *Etruscan Places* is gently humorous; and a calmness, though not a slackness, pervades the writing. It is as if the rhythms of the essays are infused with the peaceful mood of the occasion.

> There is a stillness and a softness in these great grassy mounds with their ancient stone girdles, and down the central walk there lingers still a kind of homeliness and happiness. True, it was a still and sunny afternoon in April, and larks rose from the soft grass of the tombs. But there was a stillness and a soothingness in all the air, in that sunken place, and a feeling that it was good for one's soul to be there.[3]

The young boy Albertine is described with humor and sympathy as the diminutive maître d'hôtel at Tarquinia, organizing accommodations for Japanese saltmining officials and Signori Inglesi with equal aplomb. Even an ‚insensitive and ignorant German anthropologist accompanying Lawrence to some of the tombs is described with a mellow acceptance much removed from the acerbic tone usually employed for such individuals.

The interiors of the tombs were painted with various scenes from Etruscan life, apparently imitating in the underworld the quality of the individual's previous existence. From these portrayals of feasting, dancing, and music-making Lawrence intuited a way of living and an ontology that he had tried for nearly ten years to discover.

In the easy simplicity of form manifested by the crumbling carvings on the stone tombs at Cerveteri; in the joyous celebration evident to him through the cracked and faded paintings of Tarquinia, Lawrence found at last the remnants of a model of living that would consolidate his own sense of values and buoy him up on the waters of the new voyage he was about to undertake. Studying the paintings of nobles feasting and dancing, Lawrence is struck by the spontaneity, lightness, and humor of the Etruscans, their delicate sensuality, their unassertive pleasure in the physical phenomena of their world.

> You cannot think of art, but only of life itself, as if this were the very life of the Etruscans, dancing in their coloured wraps with massive yet exuberant naked limbs, ruddy from the air and the sea-light, dancing and fluting along through the little olive-trees, out in the fresh day.[4]

In the current of attentiveness and delight of the dance Lawrence senses an attunement to mystery among those who depicted these scenes of the underworld, a sense of wonder that derives from belief.

> Behind all the dancing was a vision, and even a science of life, a conception of the universe and man's place in the universe which made men live to the depth of their capacity.
> To the Etruscan all was alive; the whole universe lived; and the business of man was himself to live amid it all. He had to draw life into himself, out of the wandering huge vitalities of the world. The cosmos was alive, like a vast creature. The whole thing breathed and stirred. Evaporation went up like breath from the nostrils of a whale, steaming up. The sky received it in its blue bosom, breathed it in and pondered on it and transmuted it, before breathing it out again. Inside the earth were fires like the heat in the hot red liver of a beast. Out of the fissures of the earth came breaths of other breathing, vapours direct from the living physical underearth, exhalations carrying inspiration. The whole thing was alive, and had a great soul, or *anima;* and in spite of one great soul, there were myriad roving, lesser souls: every man, every creature and tree and lake and mountain and stream, was animate, had its own peculiar consciousness.[5]

Death is not viewed as the visitation of the blind Furies, but as the further steps of an endless dance.

He notices that in many of the tombs the men, prepared with "the little bronze ship of death" and "all the amazing impedimenta of the important dead"—jewels, statuettes, small dishes, tools, weapons—have placed in their hands a round saucer-like object with a raised knob at the center. This is the sacred *patera* or *mundum* representing the germ of heaven and earth. Like Etruscan religion in general, the *patera* "is concerned with:

all those physical and creative powers and forces which go to the building up and the destroying of the soul: the soul, the personality, being that which gradually is produced out of chaos, like a flower, only to disappear again into chaos, or the underworld.[6]

The figure—calling to mind, incidentally, the mandala of contemplation which I suggested as a structural principle of *Lady Chatterley's Lover*—invokes in the effigy of the dead man the divine physicality of the universe, the god in change, immanent in emerging phenomena. It is the nucleus which issues forth as "red geranium and godly mignonette," and is the symbol of vitality as Lawrence describes it in *Apocalypse*. "The cosmos is certainly conscious, but it is conscious with the consciousness of tigers and kangaroos, fishes, polyps, seaweed, dandelions, lilies, slugs and men: to say nothing of the consciousness of water rock sun and stars."[7]

During 1929 Lawrence revived his correspondence with the astrologist Frederick Carter, whose manuscript "The Dragon of the Apocalypse" had so much interested him in Mexico for the potency with which, Lawrence believed, Carter had developed ancient cosmological symbols. Lawrence began in the fall of 1929 to write an introduction to Carter's cosmological study, but did not complete the work; since it was proving too long, he abandoned it, writing another, shorter introduction for Carter's book (which was not printed after all until its posthumous publication in the *London Mercury* of July 1930). In the book-length introduction, Lawrence develops, as I have elsewhere had occasion to describe, the idea of the Revelation of St. John as being originally the account of a pagan initiation ceremony, upon which was overlaid the patina of Christian instruction. He comments on his dislike of the Christianity of power:

> there are two kinds of Christianity, the one focussed on Jesus and the Command: Love one another!—and the other focussed, not on Paul or Peter or John the Beloved, but on the Apocalypse. There is the Christianity of tenderness. But as far as I can see, it is utterly pushed aside by the Christianity of self-glorification: the self-glorification of the humble.[8]

Thus the book of Revelation, he admits, had been since childhood inimical, even repulsive, to him. But he believes that the symbols of apocalypse resonate through the centuries as nodes of imaginative power. It is the symbols rather than the complete narrative of Apocalypse that Lawrence concentrates on in his study of the book of Revelation: the immanent *apokalypsis*.

He does not take on St. John's final vision of the world restored. Perhaps this is because the manuscript was unfinished; but one is tempted to affirm that it is because the renovated world had already been described in Lawrence's own terms, through the invocation of symbols of power and connection, so that his famous peroration does indeed correspond to the culminating vision of renewal which St. John describes.

Whatever the unborn and the dead may know, they cannot know the beauty, the marvel of being alive in the flesh. The dead may look after the afterwards. But the magnificent here and now of life in the flesh is ours, and ours alone, and ours only for a time. We ought to dance with rapture that we should be alive and in the flesh, and part of the living, incarnate cosmos. . . .

What we want is to destroy our false, inorganic connections, especially those related to money, and reestablish the living organic connections, with the cosmos, the sun and earth, with mankind and nation and family. Start with the sun, and the rest will slowly, slowly happen.[9]

Such rhapsodic celebration of living carries with it the equally powerful realization of sundering: "Sing the song of Death, O sing it! / for without the song of death, the song of life / becomes pointless and silly" (*Poems,* II, 723). It is only those who immerse themselves with recklessness in the running stream of temporal reality who can die in peace, as essentially a part of the flowering and fading of phenomena and now attentive to "the blue burning of the one fire."

In a late poem "Two Ways of Living and Dying," Lawrence writes of those open to "mutation in blossom" who die as they have lived, possessed by that wonder now transmuted into an inviolable peace:

> when living people die in the ripeness of their time
> terrible and strange the god lies on the bed, wistful,
>   coldly wonderful,
> beyond us, now beyond, departing with that purity
> that flickered forth in the best hours of life,
> when the man was himself, so a god in his singleness,
> and the woman was herself, never to be duplicated,
>   a goddess there
> gleaming her hour in life as she now gleams in death
> and departing inviolate, nothing can lay hands on her,
> she who at her best hours was herself, warm, flickering,
>   herself, therefore a goddess,
> and who now draws slowly away, cold, the wistful
>   goddess receding
>   (*Poems,* II, 676)

So the poet challenges his own life to be worthy in its psychic vitality to undertake the "great adventure" of death, towards which he must turn eagerly, turning "to beauty / to the breath, that is of new beauty unfolding in death" (*Poems,* II, 676).

Lawrence's abiding attention is to the psyche's attunement to the breath of the unknown. "At every moment we issue like a balanced flame from the primal unknown," he declares. "We are not self-contained or self-accomplished." In the early essay "Life" he develops the idea of such a spirit of renewal, seeing it as a visitant which one awaits with patience and courage. Transmutation must contain the destruction of that which is changed; the soul open to its destined coming to pass must suffer a letting go, a lapsing out, a little death.

> And do I fear the invisible dark hand of death plucking me into the darkness, gathering me blossom by blossom from the stem of my life into the unknown of my afterwards? I fear it only in reverence and with strange satisfaction. For this is my final satisfaction, to be gathered blossom by blossom, all my life long, into the finality of the unknown which is my end.[10]

The writer is gathered "blossom by blossom" throughout his life. I have discussed these "gatherings" as the action of apocalyptic change which the writer finds to be a powerful means of discovering relationship. Its paradigmatic formulation is the account of St. Paul's conversion on the road to Damascus: apocalyptic discovery is brought about through a kind of psychic conflagration in which the individual finds that his world is suddenly and radically remade. Such an event is explored through images of violence, trespass, or seizure.

However, as I have pointed out in regard to *Lady Chatterley's Lover,* in Lawrence's later works an increasing synergism develops, which culminates in the fully realized acceptance of change in the last poems, whose images are those of the self's cooperation with its destiny: the poet "rows" toward death; he walks through the orbits of Venus and the Sun down the long street of the stars to the gate of the moon; he lights himself with a gentian torch as he journeys down the great halls and passageways of the underworld; he hopes so to live that he is "walking still / with God, . . . now the moon's in shadow" (*Poems,* II, 723, 695-96, 697, 727).

The Etruscans, delighting in life, had a profound reverence for the wonder and mystery of death, for "the death journey and the sojourn in the afterlife." As expressive of this awe, they attended on their dead with careful ceremonies of passage, bestowing on them at their burial magnificent and appropriate accoutrements to accompany the departing spirit on its dark journey. Their kings were priests, splendid in life and invested with pomp as guides of the underworld. Yearning for such rites of passage, but lacking the structure of liturgy, Lawrence pronounces his own invocations to Hades, creates his own rites of passage, and is his own psychopomp through the long regions of the dying. The last poems are thus a triumph of synergetic power.

"Shadows," for instance, invokes the working together of bodily and natural cycles; such psycho-physical cooperation had been an abiding axiom of belief in Lawrence's work and now carries the authority of full realization. In *The White Peacock* the narrator expresses a romantic yearning for such homologous relationship between inner and outer motion, as he considers with sentimental melancholy the manifestations of spring, indifferent to the burial of the gamekeeper Hannibal. In "Shadows," on the other hand, that connection between inner and outer dissolution has none of the implicit separation of romantic analogy, but is an authoritative expression of the third presence intermediate (and intermediary) between man and nature.

> And if, as autumn deepens and darkens
> I feel the pain of falling leaves, and stems that
>   break in storms
> and trouble and dissolution and distress
> and then the softness of deep shadows folding,
>   folding
> around my soul and spirit, around my lips
> so sweet, like a swoon, or more like the drowse of
>   a low, sad song
> singing darker than the nightingale, on, on to the
>   solstice
> and the silence of short days, the silence of the
>   year, the shadow,
> then I shall know that my life is moving still
> with the dark earth, and drenched
> with the deep oblivion of earth's lapse and renewal
>   (*Poems,* II 727).

Lawrence believed consistently in the everlasting duality of light and dark, and insisted that his culture had a collectively psychic imbalance in favor of the light. He is therefore drawn often to exploration of the image of darkness, of "the mystery of the interior / where darker still than Congo or Amazon / flow the heart's rivers of fulness, desire and distress" (*Poems,* II, 607).

Darkness had powerful emotional associations for Lawrence from the early days of his childhood when he would see the colliers returning home heavily grimed from the pitface. The miners are later transformed through alchemical memory into the dark presences of such fictional characters as Will Brangwen, Ciccio, the Gypsy, Maurice the blind man, and the Pluto of "Bavarian Gentians." Lawrence writes in "Nottingham and the Mining Countryside" of the quality of powerful intimacy developed through the "butty" system of the colliers working at the coalface, each working with and looking to the safety of his partner. He sees this in relationship to the miner's sensual understanding of his environment as primarily tactile.

> When the men came up into the light, they blinked. They had, in a measure, to change their flow. Nevertheless, they brought with them above ground the curious dark intimacy of the mine, the naked sort of contact, and if I think of my childhood, it is always as if there was a lustrous sort of inner darkness, like the gloss of coal, in which we moved and had our real being.[11]

The collier's tactile perception of his world is like that of Maurice in "The Blind Man," who moves likewise in "the almost incomprehensible peace of immediate contact with darkness."

For Kate Leslie, it is in part a darkness in the eyes of the peons that calls her to remain in Mexico; she is responsive to their intimation of a different, more sensual mode of being than that in which her former rational life had been passed. Somers, in *Kangaroo*, wrestles Ben Cooley for acknowledgment of the primacy of the dark presences within the soul. "Now it is time," he insists,

> "for the spirit to leave us again; it is time for the Son of Man to depart, and leave us dark, in front of the unspoken God: who is just beyond the dark threshold of the lower self, my lower self. There is a great God on the threshold of my lower self, whom I fear while he is my glory. And the spirit goes out like a spent candle."[12]

Such is the darkness that Somers felt in Cornwall as a pre-Christian awareness, "away from the burden of intensive mental consciousness . . . back into semi-dark, the half-conscious, the *clair-obscur*, where consciousness pulsed as a passional vibration, not as mind-knowledge."[13] From this acknowledgment of what Lawrence elsewhere calls "the primeval, honourable beasts of our being" derives too his abiding insistence on the fictional exploration of strata below the conscious and the acculturated—his need to penetrate to the carbon of the self which is prior to diamond, soot, or coal.

Persistently Lawrence sees the dark as essentially passional and procreative, the haunt of the "third presence." Exploration of darkness cannot but discover fulfillment, and the final, most perfect meeting with the dark must be as a consummation. The images of "Gladness of Death" are expressive of triumph rather than loss, of completeness and flowering, rather than of distintegration:

> I shall blossom like a dark pansy, and be delighted
> there among the dark sun-rays of death.
> I can feel myself unfolding in the dark sunshine
>   of death
> to something flowery and fulfilled, and with a strange
>   sweet perfume.
>
> Men prevent one another from being men
> but in the great spaces of death
> the winds of the afterwards kiss us into blossom
>   of manhood
>   (*Poems*, II, 677).

However, the sensuality of the dark finds its most powerful expression in "Bavarian Gentians," a poem triumphant in the paradox of the transformation of the subject, dissolution, into a powerfully present image of glowing life.

In Lawrence's poem the rites of passage are celebrated as a journey to the underworld, the guide being the poet's gentian-torch. The long line and the verse's rhythmic repetition create the sense of a portentous and lengthy journey; and visual clarity is obliterated by a kinetic and tactile sensuousness. The poem grows in intensity towards its culmination, the splendid marriage of the dark god and his bride in which the narrator is participant as guest and also, in some sense, as bridegroom. The poet's marriage is with Persephone, now no longer in her generative phase but the priestess of dissolution. So the poem reveals the goddess's single nature, dissolution being but another aspect of procreation, as the writer had found that the most fruitful meetings were those in which he had encountered the darkness as the forever "other"—in sexual meeting or in non-genital sensual connection. The forked flame has here become the light of the gentian torch, the "dark of death" which is "the blue burning of the one fire."[14]

> Reach me a gentian, give me a torch!
> let me guide myself with the blue, forked torch of
>   this flower
> down the darker and darker stairs, where blue is
>   darkened on blueness
> even where Persephone goes, just now, from the frosted
>   September
> to the sightless realm where darkness is awake upon
>   the dark
> and Persephone herself is but a voice
> or a darkness invisible enfolded in the deeper dark
> of the arms Plutonic, and pierced with the passion
>   of dense gloom,
> among the splendour of torches of darkness, shedding
>   darkness on the lost bride and her groom
>   (*Poems,* II, 697).

The narrative of "Bavarian Gentians" follows a movement not unlike "Song of Death":

> how he enters fold after fold of deepening darkness
> for the cosmos even in death is like a dark whorled
>   shell
> whose whorls fold round to the core of soundless
>   silence and pivotal oblivion
> where the soul comes at last, and has utter peace
>   (*Poems,* II, 724).

Will Brangwen, in *The Rainbow,* finds himself undertaking a similar journey. Deeply in love with his newly married Anna, he finds that his life has dropped out of time into the *kairos* of pure sensual awareness; he is, mythologically speaking, in *illo tempore.*

> Inside the room was a great steadiness, a core of living eternity. Only far outside, at the rim, went on the noise and the destruction. Here at the centre the great wheel was motionless,

centred upon itself. Here was a poised, unflawed stillness that was beyond time, because it remained the same, inexhaustible, unchanging, unexhausted (*Rainbow*, p. 141).

Likewise "Jesus" discovers himself at the still center. Looking at the bowl of the starlit sky he reflects:

"How plastic it is, how full of curves and folds like an invisible rose of dark-petalled openness that shows where the dew touches its darkness! How full it is, and great beyond all gods. How it leans around me, and I am part of it, the great rose of Space. I am like a grain of its perfume, and the woman is a grain of its beauty. Now the world is one flower of manypetalled darknesses, and I am in its perfume as in a touch" (*Man Who Died*, p. 44).

Kate Leslie's desire for peace forms an image of similar configuration—entry into the still axis of the wheel, the core of the whirl, the timeless heart of the rose. Her desire is "to be alone with the unfolding flower of her own soul, in the delicate, chiming silence that is at the midst of things" (*PS*, p. 64). In "Bavarian Gentians" Lawrence imagines the long journey to Hades as entry into a living core of darkness, a sensual consummation which draws the narrator beyond the time of his dying and the slow disintegrative frustrations of the body into a timeless world, perfect in the fulfillment of desire, brought about through the motion of the symbols of the poem.

In the act of writing the poem the poet creates his ritual of passage. Invoking the marriage with Persephone, he becomes, too, the avatar of Orpheus, whose song conquered the guardians of Hades, charming them from destruction and enabling Orpheus to make the road through the underworld the passage towards eros, his love Eurydice. So the Etruscans created life in death, through the vivid, flickering grace of their painted tombs, still apparent after 2500 years. For Lawrence the transfiguring power of the imagination is his psychopomp enabling him to see with the intensity and clarity that will create the gentian flower as pure presence: the meditative counterpart of Connie's epiphany of Mellors. The flower is thus actually the torch that guides the poet towards luminous meeting. Wholly attending, he contemplates the flowers, "ribbed and torch-like, with their blaze of darkness spread blue / down flattening into points, flattened under the sweep of white day." He enters the imaginative world brought into being by the intensity of such looking, creating again that third place, neither the poet's "feeling" about the flower, nor its more objective or literal description, but another presence intermediary between dying poet and flower: the two in *illo tempore,* the burning moment in which eros eclipses thanatos, the Orphic moment of the poem.

Thus the creative will of the poet works in synergetic movement with the body's destiny, the final dissolution, but within the poem transforms that disintegration, rendering it submissive to renewal; the poet is as God creating anew the world from the cataclysmic destruction of apocalypse. "Art has two constant, two unending concerns: it always meditates on death and thus always creates life. All great, genuine art resembles and continues the Revelation of St. John."[15]

St. John's vision of universal destruction postulates for the saved a regenerate world as eternal Paradise. As I have argued earlier, Lawrence's understanding of such renewal is that, not of permanent fulfillment of desire, but of creative mutation, the mud and the heavens in the lotus. The restored world is the world continually in dissolution and renewal, blossoming with visionary suchness, dissolving to be recreated, ever in a new revelation of being. *Apokalypsis* is the intense revelation of this coming-to-be, sight restored to the pristine candor with which Adam viewed the creatures, naming each according to its own entelechy. So, as I have said, the initiate described in Lawrence's view of the narrative of Revelation dies to his own lying habit of perception and is reborn—if only momentarily, in Blake's "pulsation of an artery"—to more clarified seeing. His "third eye" is opened to the revelation of creatures living in the boundless energy of unfathomable life, each intrinsic to itself, strange and other, yet burning always with the one fire, the one life that connects phenomena surely, inexplicably, without possibility of dissolution. Thus the symbolic life of the poem is the blossoming moment of the gentian flower and the dying of the man who sees it and the life, touched into awareness of this connection, of the individual who contemplates the poem.

The phoenix had always been for Lawrence a powerful image of a self-renewal that must be initially self-destructive. Like Jesus, Lawrence held the belief that only by letting go is it possible to come to be. As Norman Mailer rightly describes Lawrence's position, "People can win at love only when they are ready to lose everything they bring to it of ego, position, or identity."[16] Time and again Lawrence explores that meeting between man and woman, between individual and environment, or of the individual with his deep self, in which submission is to the unknown, in which one yields himself and is "borrowed / by the fine wind that takes its course through the chaos of the world" (*Poems*, I, 250). The novelist likewise must abandon the old way, the psychological analysis of personality, in an attempt to reach below, to a more primal self, by

> listening-in to the voices of the honourable beasts that call in the dark paths of the veins of our body, from the God in the heart. Listening inwards, inwards, not for words nor for inspiration, but to the lowing of the innermost beasts, the feelings, that roam in the forest of the blood, from the feet of God within the red-dark heart.[17]

It is therefore impossible for the writer to imagine oblivion as separable from a new coming-to-be.

Many of the last poems, including "Bavarian Gentians," explore the intensity of the passage to darkness. In another sequence, however, the poet meditates on death in historical context, the chronology of death, finding that the diastole of sundering must in some way imply its systole, a new beginning. "Ship of Death" most bravely and powerfully enunciates this article of faith. The images central to both "Bavarian Gentians" and "Ship of Death" appear in a striking passage in *Etruscan Places.*

> Man moves naked and glowing through the universe. Then comes death: he dives into the sea, he departs into the underworld.
>
> The sea is that vast primordial creature that has a soul, also, whose inwardness is womb of all things, out of which all things emerged, and into which they are devoured back. Balancing the sea is the earth of inner fire, of after-life, and before-life.[18]

As "Bavarian Gentians" moves downward toward the core, toward the "earth of inner fire," "Ship of Death" explores the seamarks of that great ocean, home of the dolphin who leaps

> as a creature that suddenly exists, out of nowhere. He was not: and lo! there he is! The dolphin which gives up the sea's rainbows only when he dies. Out he leaps; then, with a head-dive, back again he plunges into the sea.[19]

Lawrence spent several of his last months by the ocean at Bandol, on the Mediterranean coast of France, and he wrote there a series of poems invoking the sea's power. In "Mana of the Sea," it is the undifferentiated energy of the ocean that he celebrates, energy in which the dying man has yet a part.

> And is my body ocean, ocean
> whose power runs to the shores, along my arms
> and breaks in the foamy hands, whose power rolls out
> to the white-treading waves of two salt feet?
>
> I am the sea, I am the sea!
> (*Poems*, II, 705).

In other poems he celebrates the Mediterranean as the eternally procreative womb and home of Aphrodite and Dionysus.

> This sea will never die, neither will it ever
> grow old
> nor cease to be blue, nor in the dawn
> cease to lift up its hills
> and let the slim black ship of Dionysos come
> sailing in
> with grape-vines up the mast, and dolphins leaping
> (*Poems*, 688).

In "Ship of Death" the poet meditates on the preparations needed for the voyage across the long sea, the building and furnishing of the little ship which will allow him egress from the world. He must be able to launch out upon the ocean, unlike the "unhappy dead," who linger on the shores of existence, haunted by their unfinished lives.

The process he describes is much like the self's coming to "ego integrity"[20]—that final acceptance of the events of one's life without resentment, without demand for completion or improvement. In an earlier draft of the poem, Lawrence describes in allegorical detail the necessary effort of the soul and the meaning of the accoutrements of the voyage as aspects of this "ego integrity." But in the revised poem, with more powerful generalization, the uses of the appurtenances are left unspecified:

> A little ship, with oars and food
> and little dishes, and all accoutrements
> fitting and ready for the departing soul
> (*Poems,* II, 718).

The poet meditates on timeliness, on the soul's readiness to accept the destiny of the body. Thus "Ship of Death" opens with a realization of the synchronicity of inner and outer season: "Now it is Autumn and the falling fruit." Enmeshed with that power the reader finds an awesome tenderness, as the poet—kind to himself—reflects on the soul's fear of this chill wind blowing once more "the new direction of Time."

> And in the bruised body, the frightened soul
> finds itself shrinking, wincing from the cold
> that blows upon it through the orifices.

The "fragile ship of courage" is, as the poet voyages deeper, the gradual strengthening of the will to face this new undertaking as the "adventure" of other poems in the series. The rite of passage which is "Ship of Death" is the most difficult, the invocation demanding the greatest faith, since it is the most searching—except for "Bavarian Gentians"—of the poet's experience. His initiation is to that ultimate tranquillity of the dark: "the deep and lovely quiet / of a strong heart at peace." Between his disintegrating bodily life and that absolute peace heaves the endless ocean; the naked soul shrinks from its destined venture.

As the poet has powerfully evoked the lapsing of the body at the fall of the year, so the image of the apocalyptic flood covering the face of the earth is associated with the body's dissolution. The image is, besides, a frightening evocation of the bronchial hemorrhages from which the poet was suffering, which he denied to his friends as evidence of serious illness but which are perhaps here acknowledged as symptoms of mortal sickness.

> We are dying, we are dying, we are all of us dying
> and nothing will stay the death-flood rising
> within us

> and soon it will rise on the world, on the outside
> world.

The tree of life, an image previously used by Lawrence as indicative of the self's rootedness in his world, its leaves falling and being renewed, now is destroyed, washed over in the flood tide of dissolution—the soul cowering "naked in the dark rain over the flood, / cowering in the last branches of the tree of our life."

So the poet builds his ark of faith to ride out the flood, the ark which recalls too the Etruscans' funerary ships. He takes that "dark flight down oblivion," creates the voyage as entry into the void, a meeting with the darkness previously imaged—in "Bavarian Gentians"—as consummation, but here as utter negation. Again the image of the ocean has powerful associations with the hemorrhaging life-blood of the poet.

> There is no port, there is nowhere to go
> only the deepening blackness darkening still
> blacker upon the soundless, ungurgling flood
> darkness at one with darkness, up and down
> and sideways utterly dark, so there is no direction
>   any more
> and the little ship is there; yet she is gone.

The voyager rows, but has no sense of port, nor even if there will indeed be landfall

> upon the flood's black waste
> upon the waters of the end
> upon the sea of death, where still we sail
> darkly, for we cannot steer, and have no port.
>
> Yet "out of eternity,"
>   a thread
> separates itself on the blackness,
> a horizontal thread
> that fumes a little with pallor upon the dark.

There comes to pass the strangest event in this ritual of passage—the miracle of the dawn line. The poet discovers at last the further shore; in images of consummate delicacy he envisions the little ship coming to rest.

> The flood subsides, and the body, like a worn seashell
> emerges strange and lovely.
> And the little ship wings home, faltering and lapsing
> on the pink flood,
> and the frail soul steps out, into her house again
> filling the heart with peace.

The poem, in the power and tenderness of image and movement, has brought into momentary being that pristine day which issues from the night of dissolution.

This cycle of lapse and renewal, of which death is a phase rather than a conclusion, is invoked yet once more in the late poem "Shadows." Here the poet will wake, as to a morning after sleep, like a freshly opened flower "dipped again in God and new created." For Lawrence's enduring faith is in that power beyond the will, the wind that blows through him, to which as man and writer he had been endlessly attentive. His life had been open to the immanent apocalypse brought about by such listening: to the visitation of Pan, the opening of the third eye, the coming of the Holy Ghost, the self-conflagration of the phoenix in renewal, the splitting of the rock of the Hesperides, the blinding light on the road to Damascus. Finally he creates the poems that build his fragile ship of courage, that enact his rites of passage, so that he is able to look to death as indeed another transfiguration:

> then I must know that still
> I am in the hands of the unknown God,
> he is breaking me down to his own oblivion
> to send me forth on a new morning, a new man.

Notes

Chapter 1

1. "Introduction" [to an unpublished manuscript "The Dragon of the Apocalypse," by Frederick Carter], in *Phoenix: The Posthumous Papers of D.H. Lawrence*, ed. by Edward D. McDonald (New York: Viking Press, 1936), pp. 301-2. This book of essays and other papers is hereinafter referred to as *Phoenix*.

2. The manuscript form of "The Dragon of the Apocalypse," which Lawrence read originally in 1923, was probably an early section of the book that appeared in 1926, *The Dragon of the Alchemists;* Carter's later book, on which he and Lawrence were to have cooperated, was published in 1931 as *The Dragon of Revelation.* The year before, Lawrence's original introduction to this work had been published as a separate essay, and in July 1930 his shorter introduction had appeared in the *London Mercury,* without any reference to Carter's book.

3. Frederick Carter, *The Dragon of Revelation* (Harmondsworth, 1931), Preface.

4. "Introduction," pp. 294, 297.

5. *Apocalypse,* Viking Compass Edition (New York: Viking Press, 1966), p. 18.

6. *D.H. Lawrence* (New York: Viking Press, 1973); "Lawrence and the Apocalyptic Types," *Critical Quarterly,* X (Spring 1968).

7. *D.H. Lawrence Review,* III (Fall 1970), pp. 141-60.

8. "The Metaphor of Apocalypse in the Novels of D.H. Lawrence" (unpublished Ph.D. dissertation, University of Michigan, 1973).

9. *The Utopian Vision of D.H. Lawrence* (Chicago: University of Chicago Press, 1963); *Another Ego: The Changing Views of Self and Society in the Work of D.H. Lawrence* (Columbia: University of South Carolina Press, 1970).

10. D.H. Lawrence, "Why the Novel Matters," *Phoenix,* p. 536.

11. In fact, throughout his writing Lawrence carried on a submerged dialogue with the political side of his nature; the details of this are beyond the scope of this work. A wanderer and an iconoclast, he yet complained bitterly about the frustration of his "societal instincts": he longed for rootedness, he wanted to be able to believe in affairs of the polis, but his prophetic imagination pulled him repeatedly away from the careful contemplation of political strategy towards a concern for the metapolitical question of morality and perception. Political maneuver seemed to constitute, in this view, a subsidiary activity and usually a futile one. But the dualism—expressed clearly in *Kangaroo*—is never resolved; the political writer remains at odds with the prophet.

12. For Wordsworth, the world renewed was this world.

> Paradise, and groves
> Elysian, Fortunate Fields—like those of old
> Sought in the Atlantic Main, why should they be
> A history only of departed things,
> Or a mere fiction of what never was?
> For the discerning intellect of Man,
> When wedded to this goodly universe
> In love and holy passion, shall find these
> A simple produce of the common day.

Preface to *The Excursion* (1814), quoted in Abrams, *Naural Supernaturalism*, p. 467.

13. This outline derives in the main from L.D. Clark's brief review in "The Apocalypse of Lorenzo" (in *D.H. Lawrence Review*, cited above, n.7, pp. 143-45).

14. *The Pursuit of the Millennium: Revolutionary Messianism in Medieval and Reformation Europe and Its Bearing on Modern Totalitarian Movements* (New York: Harper and Row, 1961).

15. "The Apocalypse of Lorenzo," p. 159.

16. "Why the Novel Matters," *Phoenix*, p. 533.

17. "Morality and the Novel," *Phoenix*, p. 528.

18. *The Collected Letters of D.H. Lawrence*, ed. by Harry T. Moore (2 vols.; New York: Viking Press, 1962), I, 399.

19. "Surgery for the Novel—or a Bomb?" *Phoenix*, p. 520.

20. *New Heaven, New Earth: The Visionary Experience in Literature* (New York: Vanguard Press, 1974), p. 3.

21. *Fearful Symmetry: A Study of William Blake* (Princeton: Princeton University Press, 1947), p. 8.

22. L.D. Clark, "The Apocalypse of Lorenzo," p. 158.

23. D.H. Lawrence, "On Being Religious," *Phoenix*, p. 729.

Chapter 2

1. *Letters*, I, 391.

2. Ibid., p. 378.

3. Ibid., p. 389.

4. *The Rainbow*, Viking Compass Edition (New York: Viking Press, 1961), pp. 69-70. Subsequent references—title and page numbers—will be included, in parentheses, in the text.

5. *Women in Love*, Viking Compass Edition (New York: Viking Press, 1960), "Foreword," p. viii.

6. George Ford discusses similarly the image of a germinating seed as one prevalent in Lawrence's work. *Double Measure: A Study of the Novels and Stories of D.H. Lawrence* (New York: Holt, Rinehart, and Winston, 1965), p. 107.

7. George Ford sees Ursula somewhat similarly as the biblical prophet whose life story is as if of mythic significance: an account of "the ancestry, birth, development, suffering, trial, and

triumphs of a prophet, or more accurately a prophetess, Ursula Brangwen, whose mission it will be to show the way out of a wilderness into a Promised Land." Ibid., p. 130.

8. *Studies in Classic American Literature,* Doubleday Anchor Books (Garden City: Doubleday and Company, 1955), pp. 149, 152.

9. D.H. Lawrence, *The White Peacock* (Harmondsworth: Penguin Books, 1950), p. 13. Subsequent references—title and page numbers—will be included, in parentheses, in the text.

10. In a letter dated October 18, 1910, Lawrence referred disparagingly to the novel as "a decorated idyll running to seed in realism." *Letters,* I, p. 66.

11. *Letters,* II, p. 1100.

12. "Nottingham and the Mining Countryside," *Phoenix,* p. 133.

13. *Letters,* I, p. 200.

14. Ibid., p. 282.

15. "Reality of Peace," *Phoenix,* p. 672.

16. Ibid.

17. *D.H. Lawrence: An Unprofessional Study* (Chicago: Swallow Press, 1964), p. 16.

18. "The Horse Dealer's Daughter," in *The Complete Short Stories of D.H. Lawrence,* Viking Compass Edition (3 vols.; New York: Viking Press, 1961), II, 445. Subsequent references will be included, in parentheses, in the text.

19. *Letters,* I, p. 282.

20. Early in the book Lawrence refers to "fate" and "destiny," although in a manner which suggests their use here as more or less dead metaphors; he does not subscribe to a deterministic outlook, either.

21. *Letters,* I, p. 291.

22. Eugene Goodheart compares Lawrence's technique of creating a sense of "the unwilled revelation of divinity" at such moments of crisis with the Old Testament way—as described by Erich Auerbach—of presenting events as "fraught with background," so that "the social and material texture of the narrative is a translucent medium through which divinity reveals itself." *Utopian Vision,* p. 117.

23. In the poem "New Heaven, New Earth" Lawrence describes a similar experience, in which he realizes suddenly in his wife an ineluctable otherness, not himself, a mysterious creature whose strangeness in her body's mystery kindles him to the mystery of changing being that lives at the core of life:

> Green streams that flow from the innermost continent
> of the new world,
> what are they?
> Green and illumined and travelling for ever
> dissolved with the mystery of the innermost heart of
> the continent ...

The Complete Poems of D.H. Lawrence, ed. by Vivian de Sola Pinto and Warren Roberts (2 vols.; New York: Viking Press, 1964), I, 260.

24. The elements of such a scene—wind, flower, twilight—are examples of what Eliseo Vivas calls "constitutive symbol," that "whose referend cannot be fully exhausted by explication, because that to which it refers is symbolized not only through it but in it." *D.H. Lawrence: The Failure and Triumph of Art* (Evanston: Northwestern University Press, 1960), p. 208.

25. Quoted by Richard Howard in *Alone with America: Essays on the Art of Poetry in the United States since 1950* (New York: Atheneum, 1971), p. 305.

26. Frank Kermode, *The Sense of an Ending: Studies in the Theory of Fiction* (New York: Oxford University Press, 1967), pp. 69-72, 169.

27. D.H. Lawrence, *Apocalypse,* pp. 97-98.

28. Ibid., p. 99.

29. In *Fantasia of the Unconscious* Lawrence has an interesting passage on the fear-dream of horses in which a man "suddenly finds himself among great, physical horses, which may suddenly go wild. Their great bodies surge madly round him, they rear above him, threatening to destroy him. At any minute he may be trampled down." In such a dream, he says, there may be within the dreamer a secret "yearning for the liberation and fulfillment of the deepest and most powerful sensual nature." *Psychoanalysis and the Unconscious" and "Fantasia of the Unconscious,"* Viking Compass Books (New York: Viking Press, 1960), pp. 199-200.

Chapter 3

1. *Letters,* I, p. 482.

2. Ibid., pp. 309-10.

3. Quoted by Robert Nichols in his preface to Sassoon's *Counter Attack:* Louis Untermeyer, ed., *Modern British Poetry: Mid-Century Edition* (New York: Harcourt Brace, 1950), p. 309.

4. Robert Graves, *Good-bye to All That* (rev. ed.; Garden City: Doubleday Anchor Books, 1957), p. 260.

5. *Letters,* I, p. 317.

6. Ibid., I, p. 314 (February, 1915).

7. Ibid., p. 310.

8. Lawrence tried to work out that sense of the age that is passing in the "Study of Thomas Hardy," begun in 1914 "out of sheer rage" at the war.

9. *Letters,* I, p. 366.

10. Ibid., p. 362.

11. Ibid., p. 410.

12. Ibid., p. 424.

13. Ibid., p. 453.

14. Ibid., p. 295.

15. Ibid., p. 460.

16. Ibid., pp. 375-76.

17. Ibid., p. 375.

18. Ibid., p. 466.

19. Ibid., p. 467.

20. "The Reality of Peace," *Phoenix*, p. 678.

21. *Collected Poems*, I, pp. 270-74.

22. *Women in Love*, Viking Compass Edition (New York: Viking Press, 1960), p. 5. Subsequent references will be included, in parentheses, in the text.

23. Daleski, too, points out that the structural principle of *Women in Love* is "locative"; and that "the places are related to one another not merely through a juxtaposition which yields a comprehensive view of the social scene as a whole but—so to speak—through their common location on volcanic soil." H.M. Daleski, *The Forked Flame* (Evanston: Northwestern University Press, 1965), p. 128. It is the "volcanic soil" which primarily interests Lawrence— the spiritual ferment common to the various aspects of the social scene. Social discrepancies and comparisons are less important than the spiritual malaise endemic to the complete panorama of English life.

24. *The Poetry and Prose of William Blake*, ed. David V. Erdman (Garden City: Doubleday Anchor Books, 1970), p. 544.

25. *Apocalypse*, pp. 86-87.

26. Ibid., p. 81.

27. Ibid., p. 80.

28. D.H. Lawrence, Preface to *New Poems* (American edition, 1920), in *Phoenix*, p. 219.

29. *Letters*, I, p. 341.

30. Catherine Carswell, *The Savage Pilgrimage* (London: Chatto and Windus, 1932).

31. *The Poetry and Prose of William Blake*, p. 551.

32. *Letters*, I, p. 308.

33. In his essay "*The Rainbow* and Fra Angelico," Jeffrey Meyers discusses the use Lawrence made of Fra Angelico's *The Last Judgment*, to illustrate certain ideas in *The Rainbow*, finding the painting present in the novel "both as a symbolic center of the narrative and in the biblical imagery that expresses the themes of the novel." *D.H. Lawrence Review*, VII (Summer 1974), p. 140. In this article, however, he does not develop his thesis to include discussion of the more indirect reference to *The Last Judgment* in *Women in Love*.

34. "The Reality of Peace," *Phoenix*, p. 674.

35. *Letters*, I, p. 375.

36. Ibid.

37. Ibid., p. 358.

38. Ibid., pp. 477-78.

39. *River of Dissolution: D.H. Lawrence and English Romanticism* (New York: Barnes and Noble, 1969).

40. *Letters*, I, pp. 404-5.

41. *Complete Poems*, I, pp. 212-15.

42. Stephen Miko points out that the African (or West Pacific) statue "represents a legitimate pursuit taken to its extreme, to a dead end. It is precisely because the culture it represents is

finished that the statue can capture its final sensuality. By identifying mindless sensuality with a dead civilization, Lawrence both retains his attraction to the dark powers (embodied in art, the sensuality is supreme) and rejects their more modern, destructively final embodiments." *Toward "Women in Love": The Emergence of a Lawrentian Aesthetic* (New Haven: Yale University Press, 1971).

43. *River of Dissolution,* pp. xi-xii.

44. "The Crown," in *Phoenix II: Uncollected, Unpublished, and Other Prose Works by D.H. Lawrence,* ed. Warren Roberts and Harry T. Moore, Viking Compass Books (New York: Viking Press, 1970), p. 373.

45. Ibid., p. 396.

46. "The Crown," in *Phoenix II,* p. 396. Persephone, as goddess of fruition and death, embodies such timeliness; the myth of Persephone, alluded to frequently by Lawrence, is one of his most central "fables of identity," and I shall have more to say on the myth in my discussion of *Lady Chatterley's Lover* (chapter 5). George Ford has a most interesting discussion of Lawrence's use of the Persephone myth, particularly in regard to *Sons and Lovers,* in *Double Measure,* pp. 28-47.

47. "The Reality of Peace," *Phoenix,* p. 678.

48. "The Crown," *Phoenix II,* p. 404.

49. Ibid., p. 415.

50. "Study of Thomas Hardy," *Phoenix,* p. 402.

51. Birkin's acknowledgment of the "Creative Mystery," says Baruch Hochman, is "complex, mediated through consciousness, and representing nearly total self-awareness in a mode different from ordinary civilized consciousness. It is ultimately the sensation of having one's pulse 'beat from the heart of the mystery'—a mystery that is in nature but is achieved through a yoga-like discipline of consciousness in sensuality itself." *Another Ego,* p. 39.

52. Norton Critical Edition, ed. by Thomas Moser (New York: W.W. Norton, 1968), p. 135.

53. Ibid., p. 11.

54. "The Crown," *Phoenix II,* p. 415.

55. "The Real Thing," *Phoenix,* p. 202.

56. George Ford points out that Lawrence frequently alludes, directly or indirectly, in *Women in Love* to the story of the Gadarene swine, as an expression of the devolution of culture, literally as tumbling downhill, lapsing. *Double Measure,* p. 200.

57. There is in these scenes much of that double sense experienced in reading Emily Dickinson's poetry; in poems like "I dreaded that first Robin, so" an expression of withdrawal and the denial of creative energy is transmuted into vivid, exalted life by the fierce intensity of its symbolic articulation.

58. John B. Vickery, *The Literary Impact of "The Golden Bough"* (Princeton: Princeton University Press, 1973). Prof. Vickery omits discussion, however, as to whether the parallels in substance and manner are literary borrowings or analogous thinking in Lawrence.

59. This will be an important motif in "Sun" and *The Man Who Died.*

60. *Apocalypse,* p. 137.

61. Ibid., p. 139. C.G. Jung and Lawrence are in agreement as to the primitive nature and the importance of the figure of the Woman Clothed with the Sun; cf. *Answer to Job*, trans. by R.F.C. Hull, Bollingen Paperback Edition (Princeton: Princeton University Press, 1973).

62. *Apocalypse*, p. 139.

Chapter 4

1. *Apocalypse*, pp. 109-10. The third eye corresponds in Tantric yoga to the sixth chakra, situated between the eyebrows, which, as the seat of the cognitive faculties, is associated with wisdom. Mircea Eliade, *Yoga: Immortality and Freedom*, trans. by Willard R. Trask (2nd ed.; Princeton: Princeton University Press, 1969), p. 243. As L.D. Clark attests, in *The Dark Night of the Body*, Lawrence would also have been familiar—no doubt through Pryse's *The Apocalypse Unsealed*—with the concept of the "pineal eye" of the theosophists, that pristine faculty of inner vision which, though atrophied, could be restored by the exercise of proper spiritual discipline. *Dark Night of the Body: D.H. Lawrence's "The Plumed Serpent"* (Austin: University of Texas Press, 1964).

2. "St. Mawr," in *The Short Novels*, vol. II (London: Heinemann, 1956), p. 51.

3. "Pan in America," *Phoenix*, p. 25.

4. *The Plumed Serpent* (London: Heinemann, 1926), p. 338. Subsequent references will be included, in parentheses, in the text.

5. *Aaron's Rod*, Viking Compass Edition (New York: Viking Press, 1961), p. 283.

6. Ibid., p. 146.

7. "New Mexico," *Phoenix*, p. 142.

8. Ibid., p. 143.

9. Jasscha Kessler, in "Descent in Darkness: The Myth of *The Plumed Serpent*," clearly shows Kate as the protagonist of a traditional mythic journey comprising separation-initiation-return (though the writer finds only the first two stages completed in *The Plumed Serpent*, the third to be enacted in "The Escaped Cock"). The argument details the various stages of the hero's quest: the call to adventure, the first threshold, the road of trials, the initiation. The essay demonstrates that the various events of Kate's sojourn in Mexico correspond to these mythic adventures, the object of her quest being the discovery of "wholeness of being," of life as "perpetual virginity." For Kessler the importance of the novel lies in the "drama of the hidden primal mythic adventure" below the surface of "politics and religious demagoguery." *A D.H. Lawrence Miscellany*, ed. Harry T. Moore (Carbondale: Southern Illinois University Press, 1959), pp. 239-61.

10. "On Being Religious," *Phoenix*, p. 729.

11. Lawrence describes this rootedness of self in one of the manuscript versions of the poem "Deeper than Love" as the "central primordial fire of the soul," which is

> heavier than iron
> so ponderously central, heavier and hotter
> than anything known;
> and also alone
> and yet
> reeling with connection,
> heavy with the heaviness of balance

> balance with the other, the vast unknowable fire
> that centres and balances all things.
>
> (*Complete Poems*, II, p. 951)

"Ponderously central" weight is a main theme of *Kangaroo*, as it is also of the poem "Kangaroo."

12. *Collected Letters*, II, p. 746.

13. *Love's Body*, Vintage Books Edition (New York: Random House, 1968), pp. 249, 265.

14. *Fantasia of the Unconscious*, p. 116.

15. Ibid., p. 112.

16. Ibid., p. 119.

17. Mrs. Norris is possibly, like Owen and Villiers, drawn from life. William York Tindall maintains that Lawrence's character derives from a well-known anthropologist of Mexico, Mrs. Zelia Nuttal, and that it was she who furnished Lawrence with much of the anthropological material used for his novel. *D.H. Lawrence and Susan His Cow* (New York: Columbia University Press, 1939), p. 115.

18. Edward Nehls, ed., *D.H. Lawrence: A Composite Biography* (3 vols; Madison: University of Wisconsin Press, 1957-59), III, p. 226.

19. "Study of Thomas Hardy," *Phoenix*, p. 429. Subsequent references will be included, in parentheses (with the title "Study"), in the text.

20. *Collected Letters*, I, p. 291.

21. *The I Ching, or Book of Changes*, the Richard Wilhelm translation, rendered into English by Cary P. Baynes, Bollingen Series, vol. XIX (3rd ed.; Princeton: Princeton University Press, 1967), pp. 3, 10, 11.

22. "Surgery for the Novel—Or a Bomb," *Phoenix*, p. 520.

23. *Fantasia of the Unconscious*, pp. 156-57.

24. Rudolf Arnheim, *Art and Visual Perception: A Psychology of the Creative Eye* (Berkeley: University of California Press, 1974), p. 236.

25. This capacity for being present in his activities was apparently an enduring characteristic of Lawrence—perceived by the Chambers, for instance, during Lawrence's visits to the Haggs.

> Lawrence continued to enter into the family activities, teaching the smaller children whist, cleaning the hearth for Mrs. Chambers, and peeling vegetables. He found none of the household tasks boring, and at harvest time he joined Mr. Chambers and his sons in their hayfields, four miles from the farm, opposite Greasley church; . . .
> Jessie heard her father say, "Work goes like fun when Bert's there." Another time, Mrs. Chambers remarked, "I should like to be next to Bert in heaven."

Harry T. Moore, *The Priest of Love: A Life of D.H. Lawrence* (rev. ed., of *The Intelligent Heart;* New York: Farrar, Straus, and Giroux, 1974), p. 44.

26. "Introduction" [to "The Dragon of the Apocalypse"], *Phoenix*, p. 296.

27. L.D. Clark writes eloquently of this potent image: "At the center of the circular whole, the omphalos of the book, the lake is magnetic with the stillness of a compelling eye, a cynosure like a full womb. Associated in one way or another with every significant action of the book, it

is meaningful but unfathomable. It animates all the human and natural motions that touch it, and in return receives life from them.... In the book's cosmology, the lake is, in the visible world, what the heart and eye of God are in the invisible." *The Dark Night of the Body,* p. 141.

28.   *Apocalypse,* p. 137.

29.   Ibid., p. 31.

30.   Ibid., p. 40.

31.   *The Complete Poems,* II, pp. 651-52.

32.   Ibid., p. 651.

33.   Thus Lawrence shows himself as the apocalyptist, Blake as the prophet, in the terms of a distinction made by Martin Buber in "Prophecy, Apocalyptic and the Historical Hour" in *Pointing the Way,* ed. by Maurice S. Friedman, Harper Torchbooks (New York: Harper and Row, 1963), pp. 192-207.

34.   *Love's Body,* p. 214.

35.   *The Complete Poems,* II, p. 651.

Chapter 5

1.   *John Thomas and Lady Jane* (New York: Viking Press, 1972), p. 44. Subsequent references will be included, in parentheses, in the text.

2.   The phrase is Norman O. Brown's: *Love's Body,* p. 214.

3.   *Lady Chatterley's Lover* (New York: Grove Press, 1957), p. 75. Subsequent references will be included, in parentheses, in the text.

4.   "The Real Thing," *Phoenix,* p. 202.

5.   *Mornings in Mexico,* in *"Mornings in Mexico" and "Etruscan Places"* (Harmondsworth, Middlesex: Penguin Books, 1960), p. 45.

6.   Clark notes that Lawrence's theosophical reading would have further articulated his sense of the circle: for the theosophists the circle was a symbol of perfection and godhood. *Dark Night of the Body,* p. 15.

7.   *Yoga: Immortality and Freedom,* pp. 219-27.

8.   *Collected Letters,* II, p. 843.

9.   In a fine essay on Lawrence's poetry Joyce Carol Oates develops this idea of Lawrence's resistance to analysis and conscious assessment, seeing in it a response to his continual need for subjecting the personal ego to the impersonal Other—for separating "the conscious self from the unconscious and both from the truly external, the unknown and unknowable Infinite." Joyce Carol Oates, "The Hostile Sun: The Poetry of D.H. Lawrence," in *New Heaven, New Earth: The Visionary Experience in Literature* (New York: Vanguard Press, 1974), p. 56.

10.   Bly, in an interview with Bill Moyers, speculates that since attention has been paid to the unconscious, through the study of Freud and Jung, the unconscious has responded. "For a thousand years now," Bly declares," there has only been in the West man against nature. Man is intelligent, as Descartes says, and wonderful, and nature is stupid and doesn't think and is full of snakes and alligators and so on; a naked confrontation between man and nature. What

I think has happened is that the attention to the unconscious has created a third being, which now stands between man and nature, and that's a wonderfully joyous occurrence" ("Poet at Large: A Conversation with Robert Bly," *Bill Moyers' Journal*, February 19, 1979, p. 6).

11. *Complete Poems*, II, p. 683.

12. Ibid., I, p. 256.

13. Ibid., II, pp. 666-67.

14. David Cavitch, for instance, in *D.H. Lawrence and the New World* (New York: Oxford University Press, 1969); Marguerite Beede Howe, in *The Art of the Self in D.H. Lawrence* (Athens: Ohio University Press, 1977); and Harry T. Moore, in *The Priest of Love: A Life of D.H. Lawrence*. The phrase quoted from Moore is found on page 425.

15. "The Flying Fish," *Phoenix*, p. 782. Subsequent references will be included, in parentheses, in the text.

16. Originally published by the Black Sun Press, Paris, in 1929, as *The Escaped Cock* (the title also of the original short story version of what is now Part I of the novel, published in *The Forum*, in February, 1928). Subsequent editions of the novel carried the title *The Man Who Died*. See D.H. Lawrence, *The Escaped Cock*, edited with a commentary by Gerald M. Lacy (Los Angeles: Black Sparrow Press, 1973). In my study of Lawrence I use the Heinemann Phoenix Edition text, under the title *The Man Who Died*.

17. *The Man Who Died*, in *The Short Novels*, Vol. II (London: Heinemann, 1956), p. 22. Subsequent references will be included, in parentheses, in the text.

18. Gary Snyder, "Without," in *Turtle Island* (New York: New Directions Books, 1974), p. 6.

19. "The Reality of Peace," *Phoenix*, p. 675.

20. Ibid., p. 693.

21. Interesting in this connection is Dorothea Krook's argument in *Three Traditions of Moral Thought* (Cambridge: Cambridge University Press, 1959) that Lawrence possessed a fear of loss of identity in loving and repeatedly enacted this fear in his novels. The gradual weakening of such fear, most markedly in *The Man Who Died*—Krook suggests—brought about in his writing "a corresponding weakening of the destructive element in the sexual relation and a strengthening of that kind of tenderness that drives out fear, pride and self love." *Three Traditions*, p. 285.

22. *Collected Letters*, II, pp. 745, 746.

23. Blaise Pascal, *Pensées*, trans. John Warrington, ed. Louis Lafuma (London: J.M. Dent, 1960), *pensée* number 507. In French the phrase is *"les mouvements de grâce, la dureté de coeur; les circonstances extérieures."* *Pensées*, d'après l'édition de M. Brunschvigg (London: J.M. Dent, [1913?]).

24. Daleski also makes this point about Clifford, effectively countering the critics who find that Lawrence, in portraying Clifford as physically paralyzed, weakened his case against him. Lawrence's own comment on the subject is characteristic: "I realized that it was perhaps taking an unfair advantage of Connie, to paralyze him technically. It made it so much more vulgar of her to leave him. Yet the story came as it did, by itself, so I left it alone." "A Propos of *Lady Chatterley's Lover*," in *Sex, Literature, and Censorship*, ed. Harry T. Moore, Viking Compass Edition (New Yokr: Viking Press, 1959), p. 110.

25. *Collected Letters*, II, p. 914.

26. Preface to *Chariot of the Sun,* by Harry Crosby, in *Phoenix,* p. 260.

27. *The Complete Short Stories,* Vol. II, p. 364.

28. Foreword to *Pansies,* in *The Complete Poems of D.H. Lawrence,* I, p. 424.

29. *New Heaven, New Earth,* pp. 47, 43.

30. *D.H. Lawrence and the New World,* pp. 197-99.

31. In Lawrence's work, similarly, *The Rainbow* can be seen as Ursula's growing from the Brangwens' innocence toward a fuller understanding of reality.

32. Alfred North Whitehead, *Modes of Thought* (New York: Capricorn Books, 1958), p. 27.

33. Ibid., p. 19. Whitehead makes the notion of "importance," or "valuation," a category within his discussion of creative impulse, in *Modes of Thought.*

34. Ibid., p. 161.

35. "Life," *Phoenix,* p. 697.

36. Ibid.

37. We remember Loerke's dream of the end of the world as the petrifying of all things into ice.

38. "We Need One Another," *Phoenix,* p. 190.

39. "Craving for Spring," *Complete Poems,* p. 274.

40. One of Lawrence's proposed titles for his novel was indeed "Tenderness." *Collected Letters,* II, p. 1030.

41. The vulnerability and delicate convalescence of faith in Mellors, who has been much hurt by his life, renders quite wrongheaded Cavitch's remarks on Mellors's "unflagging super-potency," in a novel of wish-fulfillment fantasy, regressive and narcissistic. The sentimentality of which he speaks would carry within it the intrinsic timbre of its falseness; *Lady Chatterley's Lover,* on the contrary, has authenticity—what Bedient finely describes as "the wonderful authority of an unwanted recovery"; its tenderness seems to be "earnest that life, given time, will prove its own physician." David Cavitch, *D.H. Lawrence and the New World,* p. 199; Calvin Bedient, *Architects of the Self: George Eliot, D.H. Lawrence and E.M. Forster* (Los Angeles: University of California Press, 1972), p. 176.

    It is apparently a fact, as Frieda Lawrence mentioned to friends, that Lawrence had been physically impotent for some while before writing his last, most "phallic" novel. If so, it would seem the more remarkable, the more courageous, to assert with such passionate conviction a belief in the power of erotic tenderness. At any event, mortally ill, he was yet able to celebrate with delight and unpossessive joy the appearance and, in their time, the passing of the "ten thousand things" that spring to life in the phenomenal world.

42. Bedient points out, too, the humor of this scene in the novel—the "almost youthful jollity" of Lawrence's characterization of John Thomas and Lady Jane—and, in general, the tone of "erotic gaiety." *Architects of the Self,* p. 178.

43. *D.H. Lawrence,* pp. 138-42.

44. "A Propos of *Lady Chatterley's Lover,*" p. 100.

Chapter 6

1. *Complete Poems*, p. 581. Subsequent references will be included, in parentheses, in the text.

2. *Etruscan Places*, p. 134.

3. Ibid., pp. 105-6.

4. Ibid., p. 136.

5. Ibid., pp. 146-47.

6. Ibid., p. 165.

7. The quotation is actually from an unpublished passage in Lawrence's notebooks unearthed by Dr. Mara Kalnins in preparing the definitive edition of *Apocalypse* and printed in *The Guardian*, October 25, 1978, p. 10.

8. *Apocalypse*, p. 16.

9. Ibid., pp. 199-200.

10. "Life," *Phoenix*, pp. 695, 698.

11. "Nottingham and the Mining Countryside," *Phoenix*, p. 136.

12. *Kangaroo* (New York: Viking Press, 1960), p. 134.

13. Ibid., p. 243.

14. *Etruscan Places*, p. 148.

15. Boris Pasternak, *Dr. Zhivago*, chapter 3; in Norman O. Brown, *Love's Body*, pp. 206-7.

16. Norman Mailer, *The Prisoner of Sex* (New York: New American Library, 1971), p. 107.

17. "The Novel and the Feelings," *Phoenix*, p. 759.

18. *Etruscan Places*, p. 150.

19. Ibid., p. 151.

20. Erik Erikson's term. Erikson describes some of the constituents of this state of mind as: "the ego's accrued assurance of its proclivity for order and meaning... no matter how dearly paid for. It is the acceptance of one's one and only life cycle as something that had to be and that, by necessity permitted of no substitutions.... In such final consolidation, death loses its sting." *Childhood and Society* (Harmondsworth: Penguin Books, 1965), pp. 259-60.

Bibliography

Works by D.H. Lawrence

Novels and Stories

Aaron's Rod. Viking Compass Books. New York: Viking Press, 1961.
The Complete Short Stories. 3 vols. Viking Compass Books. New York: Viking Press, 1961.
  Stories cited: "The Blind Man" "The Horse Dealer's Daughter" "The Man Who Loved Islands," "Sun," "The Woman Who Rode Away."
The Escaped Cock. Edited by Gerald M. Lacy. Los Angeles: Black Sparrow Press, 1973.
The First Lady Chatterley. London: William Heinemann Ltd., 1972.
"The Flying Fish." *Phoenix: The Posthumous Papers of D.H. Lawrence.* Edited by Edward D. McDonald. London: Heinemann, 1936.
John Thomas and Lady Jane. New York: Viking Press, 1972.
Kangaroo. Viking Compass Books. New York: Viking Press, 1960.
Lady Chatterley's Lover. New York: Grove Press, 1957.
The Man Who Died. In *The Short Novels.* 2 vols. London: William Heinemann Ltd., 1956.
The Plumed Serpent. London: William Heinemann Ltd., 1926.
The Rainbow, Viking Compass Books. New York: Viking Press, 1961.
St. Mawr. In *The Short Novels.* 2 vols. London: William Heinemann Ltd., 1956.
Sons and Lovers. Edited by Julian Moynahan. Viking Critical Library. New York: Viking Press, 1968.
The Virgin and the Gypsy. Harmondsworth: Penguin Books, 1970.
The White Peacock. London: William Heinemann Ltd., 1955.
Women in Love. London: William Heinemann Ltd., 1954.

Poetry

The Complete Poems of D.H. Lawrence. Edited by Vivian de Sola Pinto and Warren Roberts. 2 vols. New York: Viking Press, 1964.

Essays

Apocalypse. Viking Compass Books. New York: Viking Press, 1960.
"A Propos of *Lady Chatterley's Lover,*" *Sex, Literature, and Censorship.* Edited by Harry T. Moore. Viking Compass Books. New York: Viking Press, 1959.
Etruscan Places. "Mornings in Mexico" and "Etruscan Places." Harmondsworth: Penguin Books, 1960.

Fantasia of the Unconscious. "Psychoanalysis and the Unconscious" and "Fantasia of the Unconscious." Viking Compass Books. New York: Viking Press, 1960.

Mornings in Mexico. "Mornings in Mexico" and "Etruscan Places." Harmondsworth: Penguin Books, 1960.

Phoenix: The Posthumous Papers of D.H. Lawrence. Edited by Edward D. McDonald. London: Heinemann, 1936. Includes: "America, Listen to Your Own," "Art and Morality," "Climbing Down Pisgah," "Life," "Love," "The Miner at Home," "Morality and the Novel," "New Mexico," "Nottingham and the Mining Countryside," "The Novel and the Feelings," "On Being Religious," "Pan in America," "Poetry of the Present (Introduction to The American Edition of *New Poems*, by D.H. Lawrence)," "Pornography and Obscenity," Prefaces and Introductions to: *Cavalleria Rusticana*, by Giovanni Verga, *The Collected Poems of D.H. Lawrence, Chariot of the Sun*, by Harry Crosby, [*The Dragon of the Apocalypse*, by Frederick Carter], "The Proper Study," "The Reality of Peace," "The Real Thing," "Resurrection," "Study of Thomas Hardy," "Surgery for the Novel—or a Bomb," "Taos," "We Need One Another," "Why the Novel Matters."

Pheonix II: Uncollected, Unpublished, and Other Prose Works by D.H. Lawrence. Edited by Warren Roberts and Harry T. Moore. Viking Compass Books. New York: Viking Press, 1970. Includes: "The Crown," Foreword to *Women in Love*, "Him with His Tail in His Mouth," "Hymns in a Man's Life," "The Novel," Prologue to *Women in Love*, "Reflections on the Death of a Porcupine," Review of *The Book of Revelation*, by Dr. John Oman, "The Risen Lord."

Psychoanalysis and the Unconscious. "Psychoanalysis and the Unconscious" and "Fantasia of the Unconscious." Viking Compass Books. New York: Viking Press, 1960.

Studies in Classic American Literature. Anchor Books, Garden City: Doubleday, 1955.

"Testament III: Unpublished passages from *Apocalypse*, the last work of D.H. Lawrence." Edited by Mara Kalnins. *The Guardian*, October 25, 1978, p. 10.

Letters

The Collected Letters of D.H. Lawrence. Edited by Harry T. Moore. 2 vols. New York: Viking Press, 1962.

Letters to Thomas and Adele Seltzer. Edited by Gerald M. Lacy. Santa Barbara: Black Sparrow Press, 1976.

Works about D.H. Lawrence

Aldritt, Keith. *The Visual Imagination of D.H. Lawrence.* London: Edward Arnold. 1971.

Barr, William. "The Metaphor of Apocalypse in the Novels of D.H. Lawrence." Unpublished Ph.D. dissertation, University of Michigan, 1973.

Bedient, Calvin. *Architects of the Self: George Eliot, D.H. Lawrence, and E.M. Forster.* Berkeley: University of California Press, 1972.

Burwell, Rose Marie. "A Catalogue of D.H. Lawrence's Reading from Early Childhood." *D.H. Lawrence Review*, III (Fall 1970), 193-324.

Carswell, Catherine. *The Savage Pilgrimage.* London: Chatto and Windus, 1932.

Carter, Frederick. *The Dragon of Revelation.* Harmondsworth, 1931.

Cavitch, David. *D.H. Lawrence and the New World.* New York: Oxford University Press, 1969.

Clark, L.D. "The Apocalypse of Lorenzo." *D.H. Lawrence Review*, III (Fall 1970), 141-59.

_____. *Dark Night of the Body: D.H. Lawrence's "The Plumed Serpent."* Austin: University of Texas Press, 1964.

Clarke, Colin. *River of Dissolution: D.H. Lawrence and English Romanticism.* New York: Barnes and Noble, 1969.

Corke, Helen. *Lawrence and Apocalypse.* New York: Haskell House. 1966.

Daleski, H.M. *The Forked Flame: A Study of D.H. New York:.* Evanston: Northwestern University Press, 1965.

Delany, Paul. *D.H. Lawrence's Nightmare: The Writer and His Circle in the Years of the Great War.* New York: Basic Books, 1978.

Ford, George H. *Double Measure: A Study of the Novels and Stories of D.H. Lawrence.* New York: Holt, Rinehart and Winston, 1965.

Freeman, Mary. *D.H. Lawrence: A Basic Study of His Ideas.* New York: Grosset and Dunlap, 1955.

Gilbert, Sandra M. *Acts of Attention: The Poems of D.H. Lawrence.* Ithaca: Cornell University Press, 1972.

Goodheart, Eugene. *The Utopian Vision of D.H. Lawrence.* Chicago: University of Chicago Press, 1963.

Hochman, Baruch. *Another Ego: The Changing Views of Self and Society in the Work of D.H. Lawrence.* Columbia, S.C.: University of South Carolina Press, 1970.

Hough, Graham. *The Dark Sun: A Study of D.H. Lawrence.* London: Duckworth, 1956.

Howe, Marguerite Beede. *The Art of the Self in D.H. Lawrence.* Athens, Ohio: Ohio University Press, 1977.

Huxley, Aldous. "D.H. Lawrence" (Introduction to *The Letters of D.H. Lawrence,* edited by Aldous Huxley). *The Collected Letters of D.H. Lawrence.* Edited by Harry T. Moore. 2 vols. New York: Viking Press, 1962.

Kermode, Frank. "Lawrence and the Apocalyptic Types." *Critical Quarterly,* X (Spring 1968), 14-38.

_____. *D.H. Lawrence.* Modern Masters. New York: Viking Press, 1973.

Krook, Dorothea. *Three Traditions of Moral Thought.* Cambridge: Cambridge University Press, 1959.

Lawrence, Frieda. *"Not I, but the Wind..."* New York: Viking Press, 1934.

Leavis, F.R. *D.H. Lawrence: Novelist.* New York: Simon and Schuster, 1955.

Meyers, Jeffrey. *"The Rainbow* and Fra Angelico." *D.H. Lawrence Review,* VII (Summer 1974), 139-56.

Miko, Stephen J. *Toward "Women in Love": The Emergence of a Lawrentian Aesthetic.* New Haven: Yale University Press, 1971.

_____, editor. *Twentieth Century Interpretations of "Women in Love."* Englewood Cliffs: Prentice-Hall, 1969.

Moore, Harry T., editor. *A D.H. Lawrence Miscellany.* Carbondale: Southern Illinois University Press, 1959.

_____. *The Priest of Love: A Life of D.H. Lawrence.* Revised edition. New York: Farrar, Straus, and Giroux, 1974.

Moynahan, Julian. *The Deed of Life: The Novels and Tales of D.H. Lawrence.* Princeton: Princeton University Press, 1963.

Murry, John Middleton. *Reminicences of D.H. Lawrence.* London: Jonathan Cape, 1933.

_____. *D.H. Lawrence: Son of Woman.* London: Jonathan Cape, 1954.

Nehls, Edward, editor. *D.H. Lawrence: A Composite Biography.* 3 vols. Madison: University of Wisconsin Press, 1957-59.

Nin, Anais. *D.H. Lawrence: An Unprofessional Study.* Chicago: Swallow Press, 1964.

Rexroth, Kenneth. "Introduction." *D.H. Lawrence: Selected Poems.* Viking Compass Books. New York: Viking Press, 1959.

Sagar, Keith. *The Art of D.H. Lawrence.* Cambridge: Cambridge University Press, 1966.

Sale, Roger. *Modern Heroism.* Berkeley: University of California Press, 1973.

Spilka, Mark. *The Love Ethic of D.H. Lawrence.* Bloomington: Indiana University Press, 1955.

Stoll, John. *The Novels of D.H. Lawrence: A Search for Integration.* Columbia, Missouri: University of Missouri Press, 1971.
Tindall, William York. *D.H. Lawrence and Susan His Cow.* New York: Columbia University Press, 1939.
Vivas, Eliseo. *D.H. Lawrence: The Failure and Triumph of Art.* Evanston: Northwestern University Press, 1960.

Related Readings

Abrams, M.H. *Natural Supernaturalism: Tradition and Revolution in Romantic Literature.* New York: W.W. Norton, 1971.
Anderson, Bernhard. *Understanding the Old Testament.* Englewood Cliffs: Prentice-Hall, 1966.
Arnheim, Rudolf. *Art and Visual Perception: A Psychology of the Creative Eye.* Berkeley: University of California Press, 1974.
Auerbach, Erich. *Mimesis: The Representation of Reality in Western Literature.* Translated by Willard Trask. Doubleday Anchor Books. Garden City: Doubleday, 1957.
Blake, William. *The Poetry and Prose of William Blake.* Edited by David V. Erdman. Doubleday Anchor Books. Garden City: Doubleday, 1970.
Brown, Norman O. *Love's Body.* Vintage Books. New York: Random House, 1968.
Buber, Martin. "Prophecy, Apocalyptic, and the Historical Hour." *Pointing the Way: Collected Essays by Martin Buber.* Edited and translated by Maurice S. Friedman. Harper Torchbooks. New York and Evanston: Harper and Row, 1963.
Charles, Robert Henry. *A Critical and Exegetical Commentary on the Revelation of St. John.* New York: Scribners, 1920.
Cohn, Norman. *The Pursuit of the Millennium: Revolutionary Messianism in Medieval and Reformation Europe and Its Bearing on Modern Totalitarian Movements.* Harper Torchbooks. New York: Harper and Row, 1961.
Eliade, Mircea. *Myths, Dreams, and Mysteries: The Encounter between Contemporary Faiths and Archaic Realities.* Translated by Philip Mairet. Harper Torchbooks. New York and Evanston: Harper and Row, 1967.
_____. *Patterns in Comparative Religion.* Translated by Rosemary Sheed. Meridian Books. New York: World Publishing Company, 1963.
_____. *Rites and Symbols of Initiation: The Mysteries of Birth and Rebirth.* Translated by Willard R. Trask. Harper Torchbooks. New York: Harper and Row, 1965.
_____. *Yoga: Immortality and Freedom.* Translated by Willard R. Trask. Bollingen Paperback. Princeton: Princeton University Press, 1970.
Erikson, Erik. *Childhood and Society.* Harmondsworth: Penguin Books. 1965.
Frye, Northrup. *Anatomy of Criticism: Four Essays.* New York: Atheneum, 1968.
_____. *Fearful Symmetry: A Study of William Blake.* Paperbound edition. Princeton: Princeton University Press, 1969.
Graves, Robert. *The Greek Myths.* 2 vols. Baltimore: Penguin Books, 1955.
Jung, Carl Gustav. *Answer to Job.* Translated by R.F.C. Hull. Bollingen Paperback Edition. Princeton: Princeton University Press, 1973.
Kermode, Frank. *The Sense of an Ending: Studies in the Theory of Fiction.* London: Oxford University Press, 1967.
Mailer, Norman. *The Prisoner of Sex.* New York: New American Library, 1971.
Oates, Joyce Carol. *New Haven, New Earth: The Visionary Experience in Literature.* New York: Vanguard Press, 1974.
"Poet at Large: A Conversation with Robert Ely." Television interview, *Bill Moyer's Journal.* February 19, 1979.

Rowley, H.H. *The Relevance of Apocalyptic: A Study of Jewish and Christian Apocalypses from Daniel to the Revelation.* Rev. ed. New York: Association Press, 1964.

Tillich, Paul. *Systematic Theology.* 3 vols. in one. Chicago: Unviersity of Chicago Press, 1967.

Vickery, John B. *The Literary Impact of "The Golden Bough."* Princeton: Princeton Univiersity Press, 1973.

Whitehead, Alfred North. *Modes of Thought.* Capricorn Books. New York: G.P. Putnam's Sons, 1958.

Index